Wicked

HAMTRAMCK

Wicked
HAMTRAMCK
LUST, LIQUOR AND LEAD

VOTE COMMUNIST

Workers of Hamtramck

Against Hunger and Fascism

For Mayor—
GEORGE KRISTALSKY

Councilmen—
RICHARD RUFFINI   JENNIE ROMANIUK
CASS BAILEY   FRANK DZIUBIK
GEORGE MOSZCZYNSKI

SOBOL   For City Clerk—
MICHAEL ZACKLER

HAMTRAMCK POLICE

We Want Beer

HAMTRAMCK

GREG KOWALSKI

Wicked HAMTRAMCK

LUST, LIQUOR AND LEAD

GREG KOWALSKI

Charleston · London

THE
History
PRESS

Published by The History Press
Charleston, SC 29403
www.historypress.net

First published 2010

Manufactured in the United States

ISBN 978.1.59629.896.5

Library of Congress Cataloging-in-Publication Data

Kowalski, Greg.
Wicked Hamtramck : lust, liquor, and lead / Greg Kowalski.
p. cm.
ISBN 978-1-59629-896-5
1. Hamtramck (Mich.)--Moral conditions. 2. Hamtramck (Mich.)--History. 3. Hamtramck
(Mich.)--Social life and customs. 4. Corruption--Michigan--Hamtramck--History. I. Title.
HN80.H36K69 2010
306.09774'33--dc22
2010021955

Contents

Acknowledgements

The period photos in the work were drawn from the archives of the Hamtramck Historical Commission. Much of the background material also came from the archives of the commission. The story of kidnap victims Mary Lou Watts and Helen Gilbert recounted in Chapter 5 is reprinted with permission from the *Jackson-Citizen Patriot* newspaper. Finally, I would like to thank my greatest supporter, my mother, Martha Violet Kowalski.

Introduction

These are the tales that no one wanted told.

For years Hamtramckans have buried their past. They turned their backs on the city's often raucous and riotous history. It's understandable. The city was the subject of bad publicity, even attaining national notoriety, for its lurid tales of graft, bootlegging and all manner of corruption.

These stories often overshadowed the significant contributions Hamtramckans made to the fields of labor, education, arts, sports and more.

Indeed, Hamtramck's 1927 public school code was so progressive that it served as a model for schools around the nation. But who wanted to read about that when there was a juicy story about a gangland slaying to dress up the front page?

Nor was that type of thing even the norm. Everyday Hamtramckans struggled with the deprivations of the Great Depression and sacrificed so much of what they had to build magnificent churches like St. Florian, where students in the adjacent school bought bricks for the church at a penny apiece. It may not seem like much today, but it was a major sacrifice then.

So when a string of Hamtramck's leading politicians was tossed into prison on corruption convictions—and brothels, speakeasies and blind pigs came to characterize much of the town—the good folks of Hamtramck did not want to be reminded of them once they were swept away and replaced with clean government in a law-abiding community.

Little was written about Hamtramck's lively past. Most documents relating to those days were destroyed, memories faded and the principal characters died. Sadly, they and what they did—bad and good—drifted into obscurity.

That's just not right.

Hamtramck wasn't built just by the good. The bad and the ugly also played a key role in forging this industrial town. And their stories deserve to be preserved and recounted.

We shouldn't revel in tales of corruption but we can understand how they came to happen in a different time under specific circumstances that were far more complicated than may seem at a casual glance.

Modern Hamtramck was made to a great extent by the large Polish immigrant population that flooded into town between 1910 and 1920. They brought their own traditions, customs and deep faith in the Catholic religion with them when they came to Hamtramck. So when the American government—that was already foreign to them in so many ways—deemed that the manufacture and sale of alcoholic drinks was illegal, they weren't about to turn off their mighty thirst for a good *pivo* (beer).

Prohibition was absurd, in their view. Most Americans came to feel that way, too. But for the Poles, there was nothing immoral about sipping a beer. Yet in Hamtramck, as it did around the country, Prohibition spawned a level of corruption that did far more harm than whiskey ever did.

These folks did not think they were being all that bad as they made their barrels of bathtub gin—in their bathtubs.

Of course, not all of Hamtramck's problems related to Prohibition, and many of the characters who ended up charged with corruption were genuinely lousy people. For the most part, they got what they deserved, a stay in jail or worse.

But they, too, played a role in Hamtramck's history and should be remembered, not in any sense of honor, but as players in the story of our town.

And what a story it is. It is a tale filled with high drama and low comedy; of pathos and tragedy; of honor and betrayal.

It's a wicked tale, indeed.

CHAPTER 1
Trouble Brewing

As he stood on the railroad tracks, the tall weeds swayed and shimmered in the summer heat. The tracks made a pair of silver lines that converged and quickly were enveloped in the countryside. It was hot, dry and desolate—almost.

It was perfect.

"This is the spot," John Dodge thought as he surveyed the sparse countryside. Or maybe it was Horace. Likely it was both. We don't know exactly what the Dodges said as they made their choice for a site to build their new factory. But their reaction to what they saw in the summer of 1909 was satisfaction and confidence that this was an ideal spot for what they envisioned.

And so began the modern history of Hamtramck. At that time, Hamtramck was a dusty village of about 3,500 people, mainly German farmers and saloonkeepers. There were a few factories pushing smokestacks above the fields, but little else. Most of the stores and saloons in town clustered along Jos. Campau Avenue, mainly south of Holbrook Avenue. Judge Merique's courthouse was a wooden shack, and the entire police department consisted of one man, Barney Whalen. It's difficult to believe even the Dodges knew what they were about to do to Hamtramck—for better and for worse.

Not much progress was evident, although Hamtramck was already 112 years old by this time. For most of its existence, Hamtramck's single greatest accomplishment was to serve as a landscape buffet for the city of Detroit, which routinely sliced off portions of it to add to its own territory. The losses didn't seem to be mourned by anyone, and it looked like the memory of Colonel John Francis Hamtramck was headed for inevitable oblivion.

John and Horace Dodge built modern Hamtramck, turning it from a dusty farming village to a major city in the space of a decade. Their massive factory drew thousands of immigrants to work in Hamtramck. *Courtesy of Walter P. Reuther Library, Wayne State University.*

The carved memorial to him remained in place in Mount Elliott Cemetery, yet he was known only to historians long after his death in 1803. And Hamtramck, the village, was a remnant of what it had been.

Hamtramck had appropriated the colonel's name for his commendable service to the Continental Army and later with the early American forces. This was made more notable because Colonel Hamtramck was actually born Jean Francois Hamtramck in 1756 in Montreal, Quebec, Canada. He grew up with a hatred of the British who occupied his homeland, so he came south of the border when the American Revolution began to join the American army in New York.

Changing his name to John Francis, Hamtramck rose to the rank of colonel and distinguished himself. He was not bound for greatness, but he was a solid soldier who could be relied upon to do his duty well. Following the Revolutionary War, he remained in the military as the Americans wrestled with the pesky British who refused to withdraw from the western territories. Although they had lost the war, they remained on the fringes of the frontier, harassing the Americans whenever and wherever they could.

Finally fed up with the British, President George Washington sent troops to the west—which then meant Michigan, Ohio, Illinois and Indiana—in the 1790s to finally oust them. Hamtramck served under General "Mad" Anthony Wayne and established Fort Wayne in Indiana.

On July 11, 1796, two ships carrying sixty-five men under the command of Colonel Hamtramck arrived at Detroit to accept the surrender of the British, although it might not be proper to characterize it as that. The British basically just walked away.

Two years later, Hamtramck Township was created, bordering the city of Detroit and extending into the wilderness later known as the 10,000 Acre Tract.

After Colonel Hamtramck's death, all of his possessions, which had been kept in storage, were destroyed in the fire of 1805 that virtually extinguished Detroit. As a result, no portraits of Hamtramck exist, so we only have references of him being a rather short man who made a somewhat comical figure on his large horse. Yet he was an accomplished soldier and well respected by those who knew and served with him. After his death, he was interred in the cemetery at St. Anne's Church and then later moved to Mount Elliott. A restless soul after death, he was moved for presumably the final time—with great ceremony—to the City of Hamtramck in 1962, where he is buried in Veterans Memorial Park. Appropriately he rests under the war monument that lists the names of every Hamtramckan who died in our nation's wars going back to World War I.

But other than his name, and the presence of what remains of his body, Colonel Hamtramck was as foreign to what Hamtramck would become as an eighteenth-century figure could be. But Hamtramck the man and the town were products of their time. After his distinguished career in the military, Colonel Hamtramck retired to the Detroit area, and in his honor the first Hamtramck Township was formed in 1798. It stretched from the Detroit River to Base Line—which would later become known as Eight Mile Road—and from Woodward Avenue on the west through the Grosse Pointes on the east. The Grosse Pointes would split off in 1848, and the township as a whole would almost immediately begin a long history of disappearing. As Detroit grew, it annexed portions of the township bit by bit until the last portion vanished in the 1920s, well after the city of Hamtramck was formed.

Through the nineteenth century, Hamtramck Township was for the most part a rural area, with some industry clustered along the Detroit River. The Detroit Stove Works grew to be one of the largest stove manufacturing companies in the world and likely was the largest business ever in the township. But it certainly wasn't the only one.

The *Detroit Post* newspaper of August 13, 1869, carried a long story on the industrialization of Hamtramck; it captured the essence not only of what that tiny portion of Hamtramck had become but foreshadowing what greater Hamtramck would come to be as a whole.

"A cloud of smoke hanging on the south-eastern potion of the city marks the iron manufacturing quarter of Hamtramck," it began. The article then related that while there may have been some questions about the dangers of air pollution (a concern even at that time), the growing iron industry was bringing prosperity to the metro area. Long before auto plants appeared, the hunger for iron was great. And Michigan could produce it. The iron ore mines in northern Michigan unearthed the product, and Detroit—strategically located among the Great Lakes—became a hub of transportation and, later, manufacturing.

The *Detroit Post* article noted:

> *The iron ore of Lake Superior was just then coming prominently into notice, and these works did much toward the introduction of the iron. Its superior quality for various kinds of work has now been definitely established, and the furnaces of Hamtramck are annually producing large quantities of it, manufacturing it and sending it to all parts of the country. Where were then orchards and green fields, stretching down to the pleasant banks of the river, are now docks, loaded with coal and iron, warehouses filled with manufacturers, and furnaces and foundries whose smokestacks blacken the face of the sky, while below are runs of liquid fire, and swarms of grimy workmen in action here and there.*
>
> *A village has grown up about these establishments, to which fifteen or twenty dwellings have been added during the present year. Most of these houses are occupied by workmen in the shops, and grocery and other stores have sprung up to supply the town with the necessities of life.*

Significantly, the story noted, "The improvements of that portion of the town has resulted entirely from the prosperity of the iron manufacturing establishments there located."

Iron: it would forge Hamtramck, but not yet.

At this point, the industry and workers that supported it were mainly clustered along the banks of the Detroit River. North of Jefferson Avenue, the landscape was decidedly rural but changing. In December, 1869, the *Detroit Advertiser* said that area of Hamtramck "is fast growing as a choice spot for suburban homes." That was probably the first and last time Hamtramck has ever been referred to as an example of suburban living. In fact, farms, orchards, creeks and railroad lines were the principal features that one would see as they went north into the township.

Along the Detroit River, however, Hamtramck was developing into quite a cosmopolitan area. In June 1905, the *Detroit News-Tribune* ran an extensive story on the community, noting "from a wilderness of 60 years ago, Hamtramck has grown to be one of the greatest manufacturing districts in the city, as well as an amusement center."

The story recounted how factories were springing up in the township. "Among the largest factories are several which employ as many as 2,000, and at present the Morgan & Wright, Co., the largest producers of rubber goods in the country are planning to locate their main plant in what was once the sleepy (township) of Hamtramck."

Oddly, it was during this period that Hamtramck developed a reputation as somewhat of a recreation center. Clustered along Jefferson Avenue at the river were about twenty-six amusement venues including dance halls, skating rinks, merry-go-rounds, shooting galleries, bowling alleys and pool halls.

The story related:

> *On summer evenings the scenes about these places are of considerable interest. At about 7 o'clock the rush begins and from then until 1:30 there is a steady stream of people coming and going. Car after car stops at the (Belle Isle) bridge, leaves its passengers and goes on to the end of the line practically empty. From the time the resorts open for the evening people mingle in old Hamtramck as they would nowhere else in the city.*

But it was industry—not amusement—that had the greatest impact on shaping the future of Hamtramck.

Long before the Dodges came to Hamtramck, the presence of railroad lines drew William L. Davies and Thomas Neal to a certain site in Hamtramck Township that would later form a part of the village of Hamtramck. In around 1896, Davies and Neal bought a piece of land on St. Aubin Avenue crossed by the Michigan Central Railroad tracks. They had tapped into the growing Detroit housing market several years before when they established their Acme White Lead and Color Works paint factory. In the beginning, it was just the two of them working up to eighteen hours a day, launching their company. But when the orders started flowing in, they soon were able to expand their operations, hiring more workers and looking for something larger than their first forty-foot by seventy-foot factory building.

Originally called the Acme White Lead Paint Company, this factory actually predated Dodge Main by nearly two decades. It was one of the first factories in what would become the Village—and later City—of Hamtramck.

Foreshadowing the Dodges, they seemed to follow the railroad lines to Hamtramck, beginning construction on what would become a massive paint manufacturing factory. Within a few years, 1,000 people were employed at the plant producing paint, lacquer, varnish and enamel. Big business had arrived in town, despite the fact that it was still mainly a land of fields and ditches, creeks and forests.

In the coming years, a few more heavy industries would move into the area, precursors of the flood that would occur after the opening of the Dodge Main factory. From the American Electric Heater Company at Dequindre and Carpenter Streets at the far north end of town to Swedish Crucible Steel and Michigan Smelting and Refining Company in the south, the mold of industrial Hamtramck was being poured.

In 1900, a group of Hamtramckans including C.A. Fields, W. Dickinson, H. Mueller and J. Hawkins met at Holbrook School, which had been built just a couple of years earlier, to discuss the possibility of establishing the Village of Hamtramck. Their aim was to preserve the identity of Hamtramck, which was being steadily eroded by the expansion of Detroit. They turned for help to state senator Seneca C. Thaver, who was developing a reputation

16

Right: The gravestone of Johann George was unearthed at the Dodge Man site as the old factory was being demolished. Mr. George died on September 28, 1886, but that's all that is known about him. He likely was one of Hamtramck's early German settlers.

Below: Al Ziskie's Bar was a typical watering hole in the village of Hamtramck in 1912. Note the pail, likely for beer, that one of the customers (known as *stamgasts*, or bar patrons) is holding.

17

for organizing townships and villages. Thaver embraced the task and the town. He soon completed the legal procedures to facilitate incorporation, which was enthusiastically received by the locals. Thaver apparently liked Hamtramck so well he became the village's first attorney and later served as Hamtramck's first city attorney following incorporation. In 1901, the Village of Hamtramck officially came into being, carved from a 2.1-square-mile section of Hamtramck Township.

On August 26, 1901, the first village election was held. Anson C. Harris was named village president; Henry M. Jacobs was clerk; Henry Krause, assessor; John Heppner, treasurer; and William Hawkins, Ernest Oehmko, Henry Mueller, Joseph Segrist, John Berres and Martin Wojcinske, trustees.

Tellingly, one of the first actions of the new council was to authorize an application for a $1,000 loan for the village. And thus began a pattern of questionable budget practices that would continue for decades. The council did, however, begin looking into doing some needed improvements, like installing water lines and street lights. The Village of Hamtramck essentially grew from the south end and advanced north. That is, the earliest businesses and houses, with the exception of some of the farm houses like the Dickinson and Dolland Farms, were clustered along Jos. Campau south of the Holbrook Creek. That creek, at the bottom of a ravine, was a key feature of the village and posed a serious safety threat in winter when people complained about being blown down its icy slopes by the wind.

Hamtramck's population stood at about 1,500 people. In 1931, Frank Shultheis, custodian at Copernicus Junior High School, wrote down his recollections for the school bulletin, which gave a first-hand picture of Hamtramck at this time. He wrote:

Not many of those who view the thickly populated area of Hamtramck, with its paved streets and sidewalks today, can visualize the great willow swamp which was the Hamtramck of but a few years ago.

There was a country ditch along Holbrook Avenue, 20 feet wide and 12 feet deep, with a bridge crossing it at the intersection of Jos. Campau Avenue. During the spring thaws, when the water was high in the ditch, the fish would come up to spawn. Often I would stand where the Peoples Wayne County Bank is now (southeast corner of Holbrook and Jos. Campau) and using a pitchfork as a spear, would get enough fish in a short time to supply our table.

There was a high board fence on the west side of Jos. Campau Avenue, running from Holbrook to Caniff. In the winter the snow would blow through the fence and pile on the road in such high drifts that I would have to drive my team through where the alleys are now.

Coming along Holbrook Avenue at that time of year, one was always in great danger of being swept into the deep ditch. The citizens of Hamtramck in those days would walk along beside their horses, trying to keep the sleigh from skidding into the water, for fear of sliding in with the team and sleigh at some very slippery place. On one or two occasions I have felt very uncomfortable as I tried to get horses, harness, and sleigh untangled, while standing knee-deep in icy water.

The only store in town was on the corner of Jos. Campau Avenue and Alice Street. There was a frame building at the corner of Holbrook Avenue and Jos. Campau that the farmers called 'The Coffee Mill.' This marked the halfway point to Detroit.

To reach my barn in the spring (my house was right where the Junior High School building is now) I would often have to walk out on a makeshift bridge built of boards placed upon saw-horses. Where the Senior High School building now stands (Hewitt Street) was a cornfield. In plowing up this field for the excavation of that building I lost my gold initial ring. So,

It was the rail lines that brought John and Horace Dodge to Hamtramck. This contemporary scene is close to what the Dodges saw when they considered locating their factory here.

somewhere underneath the building in which I work is my ring, and I have just about given up hopes of ever finding it.

If Hamtramck changes as much in the next fifteen years as it has in the last fifteen I wouldn't imagine what it would become.

The Hamtramck that Shultheis remembered began to disappear in 1910 when John and Horace Dodge stood alongside the railroad tracks.

They followed a long road to get to Hamtramck that took some fascinating turns.

John Dodge was born in 1864, and Horace arrived three years later. They spent their early lives in Niles, Michigan, before moving to Battle Creek, then Port Huron and finally to Detroit in 1887. John found work in the Murphy Iron Works and was soon joined by his younger brother. In 1892, the brothers took a job with the Dominion Typographic Company in Windsor, Ontario, Canada. By this time the brothers already had formed an inseparable bond. They worked together—and they drank together. In time they would become known as really bad boys for their antics, including some very public drunken brawls. But in these early years, they stayed mainly out of trouble, keeping company with each other. It was during this period that Horace developed an improved bicycle bearing that provided a smoother ride. They patented the bearing and went into business on their own, manufacturing bicycles incorporating the bearing.

In 1900, the Dodges opened their own machine shop on Beaubien Street in Detroit, and officially began doing business as the Dodge Brothers. They had expanded their skills and range to build and repair machinery, including engines. The Dodge Brothers were establishing a reputation as first-rate engineers, so much so that, in 1901, Ransom E. Olds contacted them to produce engines and later, transmissions, for his Olds runabout. The Dodge Brothers expanded their interests in the auto industry in 1903 when they agreed to supply auto components to Henry Ford for his Fordmobile.

From the start, the working relationship with Ford was a sour one. There were problems over payments, with Ford quickly falling behind in what he owed the Dodges. Even so, the Dodges expanded their services for Ford, supplying an increasing range of parts. As orders increased, the money rolled in, at least when they could get Henry Ford to pay them. But they also began to receive a generous amount of income on dividends from Ford stocks they had acquired. In 1904, the Dodges expanded their operations with a new 90-by-180-foot building on Monroe Avenue in Detroit. Soon even that wasn't enough to keep up with the growing demand for their components.

They leased additional space in a building on Rivard Street, and their staff expanded to some 1,000 employees. Still, they needed more space.

In 1909, it was announced that the Dodge Brothers had bought a twenty-four-acre piece of land in Hamtramck for $100,000. Noted architect Albert Kahn was hired to design the new factory, which would include offices, a forge, powerhouse and machine shop. By 1911, a substantial portion of the complex was complete. Kahn was likely the leading industrial architect of his time, but for reasons that aren't clear his performance for the Dodges was subpar. The brothers complained about the quality and timeliness of some of the work. Failing to get satisfaction from Kahn, the Dodges turned to the firm of Smith, Hinchman & Grylls for work done after 1912.

In any case, the complex of buildings that collectively become known as Dodge Main would stand solidly as one of the largest plants in the world. It was an often-curious blend of massive, steel-reinforced columns, wood-block floors and some building that looked like it belonged in a stately English garden. Although the first buildings were up by November of 1910, the first cars wouldn't roll off the production lines until 1914.

By then the Dodges had had enough of Henry Ford and the difficulties of working with him, although they weren't ready just yet to end their lucrative relationship with him. Initially, the Dodges earned little from their Ford stock

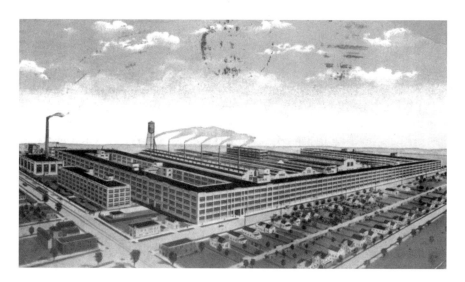

A 1915 postcard shows the Dodge Main factory just a year after it produced its first car. It would grow much larger than the view depicted here. Jos. Campau runs diagonally along the lower-left corner of the picture.

dividends. But as Ford's fortunes improved, so did the stocks; and the Dodges were earning millions of dollars by 1908. Working with Ford they had also gained a wealth of experience building car components. They were confident they could build their own cars and would be free to make design changes and improvements as they saw fit. A lot of people shared in the Dodges' confidence. When the brothers announced they were going to build and sell cars, they were flooded with requests from would-be dealerships across the country. The Dodges built a huge franchise network and promoted their products in an effective advertising campaign.

In July 1913, the Dodges gave Henry Ford a year's notice that they would cease supplying him with parts for his cars. The stage was set for the launching of a legendary branch of automobiles—and for the creation of modern Hamtramck.

There likely was a lot of nervous talk at Muenchinger's restaurant as the walls of the new Dodge factory were going up just down the muddy street. Muenchinger's, a two-story wooden structure on Jos. Campau near the railroad tracks, was the unofficial political center of the village. More bar than restaurant, it characterized the primary form of business that made up early Hamtramck. By the 1890s, bars like Cooper's saloon on Jos. Campau were flourishing, steadily serving the *stamgasts*, or patrons. In 1904, saloon permits were granted to J.P. Kaiser, A.P. Schroeder, M. Kulczynski, J.C. Adams, L. Becker, F. Bohn as well as Mr. W. Muenchinger. These were the places where Hamtramck's powerbrokers gathered. In 1901, the Village of Hamtramck's several hundred residents were mainly German farmers and shopkeepers. Over the next decade, the town grew substantially but still was relatively small, with about 3,500 residents in town in 1910, still mainly of German descent. A few prominent citizens like Michael Grajewski and W. Lukasiewicz sported Polish names, but more had names like Charles Faber and R. Van Eeckout.

Until 1910, the Germans had no trouble maintaining political control of the village. But with the opening of Henry Ford's auto plant in nearby Highland Park in 1909 and the Dodge factory the following year, the call went out for workers. Soon new residents were pouring into Hamtramck, and almost all were of Polish descent. Some came straight from Poland; others first worked in the mines of Pennsylvania; and still others lived and worked just south of Hamtramck in the old Poletown section of Detroit clustered around St. Albertus Church at St. Aubin and Canfield Streets. Some were skilled tradesmen, while others knew nothing more than how to

This is believed to be a portrait of an immigrant family. It captures the hard, often-colorless life of the drudgery the families faced.

plow a field. Regardless of whatever social status any of the immigrants had, they shared a desire to build a better life, even if that meant working in the grueling conditions of the auto factories.

And so they came in vast numbers. From 3,500 people in 1910, Hamtramck's population swelled to 48,000 in 1920. It was one of the fastest-growing, most densely populated towns in America with an astounding 24,000 people per square mile. And that number would continue to rise to 56,000 by 1930. For the original Germans, this was an alarming turn of events. In 1901 when the village was formed, Germans made up about 95 percent of the population. By 1915, that number shifted strongly toward the Poles, who then made up 80 percent of the population.

Still, the Germans managed to hold on to power. They were helped at first by the Poles' failure to assimilate. Many didn't become citizens, so they couldn't vote. And what few were able to vote had to overcome obstacles put into place by the village council, like the practice of abruptly closing the polls at 4 p.m. on election day, just before the auto workers' day in the factory ended.

The lack of a voice in local affairs was recognized as a problem by some civic-minded Poles who attempted to have the Hamtramck Public Schools hire a teacher to help Americanize their countrymen. But the school board, which had only one Polish member, rejected the proposal. However, some support did come through the Tau Beta Community House. Tau Beta was a social organization founded in 1901 by four fifteen-year-old Detroit girls. They were rich kids attending University Liggett High School, looking for an excuse to party. In order to legitimize themselves, they started dabbling in charitable work by linking with the Visiting Nurse Association. As more girls became involved in Tau Beta, they began to extend their reach, which led them to Hamtramck, where there was a rapidly growing need for all manner of social services. In 1916, the Tau Beta girls opened up their first community house at 159 Hanley Street. Known as the house with the light because of its burning porch light, it was a typical neighborhood home of the time. It was described by the Tau Betans as "a two-family structure which differed externally in no way from dozens of other houses on many streets in the Village of Hamtramck."

Most Hamtramckans were very hard working. They spent long hours in the Dodge Main plant and other factories for little pay.

Tau Beta Community House was founded in 1901 by four fifteen-year-old Detroit girls. Seeing a desperate need for social services, the organization came to Hamtramck in 1916, first operating out of a house on Hanley Street. It was replaced by this building, which was used until 1927 when the big community house across the street was opened.

So not only was the neighborhood unimpressive, it was even oppressive. Mildred Plumb described it in Tau Beta's history, published in 1938: "Cheaply constructed houses and duplexes were springing up in dozens on unpaved streets. There were, for a long time after we entered the community, large numbers of vacant lots, but there were no playgrounds. The school system was undeveloped, the village government had little vision of the public's needs, and naturally was in no hurry to supply what it did not recognize as essential."

One of Tau Beta's first acts was to use $26.10 in donations to supply Christmas dinners for six families whose names had been provided by the Hamtramck Poor Commission. Viewed suspiciously at first by the immigrant population, Tau Beta soon won the support of the community. By 1918, it was providing a wide range of services, including calling doctors, helping with insurance questions, distributing food baskets, taking kids on picnics and building a playground. During the great flu epidemic of 1918, Tau Beta helped the board of health with the increased paperwork related to the growing number of cases. Tau Beta also established the Hamtramck Public Library and began to work with Hamtramck Public Schools to conduct programs in the school buildings.

As the 1910s grew to a close, Tau Beta took on two problems that threatened the fabric of the city. One was juvenile delinquency, which was not uncommon in any poor community. Tau Beta countered the problem by offering a host of activities to young people, including theater productions. But the other issue was perhaps unique to Hamtramck. The Russian Revolution had ushered in Communism there in October 1917, and it wasn't long before the Communists were coming under increased scrutiny in the metro Detroit area, as they were across the nation. In Hamtramck, the longtime resident Germans viewed the new Polish immigrants suspiciously as Bolsheviks.

Few of the Poles had anything to do with the Communists. And as for the Russian connection, many Polish men fled to America to avoid being drafted into the Russian army during the days of the czar. Tau Beta quickly recognized that the Poles needed to be Americanized. Tau Beta never embraced politics of any sort, but it did facilitate citizenship classes and strove to promote the American way through its many programs—which it did until the organization closed shop in Hamtramck in 1958, deeming that by then it could not provide any more than the city government and schools already were by that time.

Tau Beta played a significant role in building modern Hamtramck and, to some degree, helped motivate the new residents to become politically active.

The Germans took note of the rising number of Poles. Rather than giving up political power, as appeared inevitable, the German political leaders put out feelers to the City of Detroit, proposing that Hamtramck be annexed. The local Poles were outraged. To fight the annexation threat, they formed the American-Polish Political Club and began to attend the village council meetings. They began publishing a Polish-language weekly newspaper, *Kurjer Hamtramicki,* to inform the Polish community of what was going on in village hall. They further pushed the village government to hire a Polish-speaking clerk in the village clerk's office to help with the mainly Polish-speaking population.

Finally flexing their muscles, the Poles defeated a measure to allow Hamtramck to be annexed by Detroit. But that wasn't enough. The German minority still controlled the village and the township, both of which imposed taxes on the residents. Feeling overtaxed and underpowered for so long, the Poles gained momentum from their victory over annexation. They now understood the power of the ballot and what they could accomplish by becoming citizens and registering to vote. In 1921, they proved that again in the most dramatic manner. The question of incorporating as a city was put to a vote. The turnout wasn't large, but it was decisive. Of the 1,110 votes cast, 870 were in favor of becoming a city. The death knell had sounded for the power of the Germans. Along with voting for incorporation as a city, a city charter commission had been elected. The names of the nine members of the commission were telling: P. Krause, J. Dzwonkiewicz, A. Nowakowski, S. Travers, C. Plagens, M. Kulcznik, S. Bloch, M.A. Wosinski, P. Matyniak and F. Marecki. Almost all were Poles. The draft of the city charter was sent to the state capital in January 1922, where it gained quick approval. The first city election was set for April 3, 1922. The results were a curious mix brought about by the intense politicking leading up to the vote. The African American population of Hamtramck wasn't large at this point, but it was active. And every vote mattered, so all the candidates wooed the African American residents. In the process, Dr. James L. Henderson, a prominent African American, was among those elected to the city council. However, he was not a pioneer; another prominent African American, Ordine Toliver, had served on the last village council. Also elected in 1922 was Peter C. Jewzewski as mayor; Andrew Templeton, Casimir Plagens and Walter Gaston as councilmen; Joseph Mitchell as city clerk; Walter Merique as treasurer; and Stephen Majewski and Walter Phillips as justices of the peace.

Bigger changes were coming. By the next election, in 1924, virtually every person elected to office had a Polish name.

In a way it was the culmination of a process that actually began in 1910 when the Dodge Brothers began building their factory. Even as the massive plant opened, it began expanding and eventually would cover five million square feet of floor space on 135 acres of land. Whole streets, like Bismarck and Whiting, would be swallowed by the factory. Its thundering forges would come to symbolize Hamtramck's heartbeat, and the growing streams of workers pulsing in and out of the plant were the blood of the factory and the town itself.

Hamtramck was growing fast. Whole neighborhoods were being thrown up at a furious rate as houses were built to accommodate the workers. Maximizing what was available, developers put up single and multifamily houses and even boardinghouses on lots barely 30 feet wide by 100 feet deep. Hamtramck's rural character was draining as fast as Holbrook Creek was turned into a main street. Even DeWitt C. Holbrook's farm on the north side of the creek was plowed and then paved over. And the

Long before urban renewal programs began, decrepit houses littered the city. This one was on Leuschner Street—later known as Miller Street—next to Dodge Main. Its styling was typical for an immigrant family.

transformation wasn't just from rural to urban; it was from cornfields to concrete. It was profound, traumatic change perhaps unique in the history of America. Certainly other towns have evolved radically over time—even New York City was once forests and meadows. But its change to a city of skyscrapers took decades, even centuries. Hamtramck reconstituted itself in just a few years.

The rapid change was as traumatic as it was dramatic. And it may be a key reason that Hamtramck started steering a new course, one that would take it on a wild ride on the wild side of life the likes of which were hardly seen anywhere else in America.

CHAPTER 2
Still Life

It was called the Noble Experiment, but it wasn't—at least not in Hamtramck. In fact, it didn't make any sense at all. What could be wrong with having a glass of beer, something that Poles had done for centuries in the Old Country?

But this was America, and for decades a movement was building to rid the nation of Demon Rum. It picked up a lot of momentum in 1893 with the founding of the Anti-Saloon League in Ohio. The movement pushed prohibition laws in individual states with the goal of drying up America. Michigan was a bit ahead of the nation as a whole, approving a statewide prohibition of the sale of beer, wine and liquor in 1916. The law was to take effect on May 1, 1917.

Hamtramck at this time was a rapidly growing industrial town. The Dodge Main factory had been producing cars for three years. The factory already was taking on massive proportions as more workers were hired. The surrounding village was rapidly losing what was left of its rural atmosphere. Indeed, the very air was changing with the proliferation of belching smokestacks. The population was heading toward 50,000, mainly Polish immigrants who had come to Hamtramck to work at Dodge Main. They brought a mighty thirst with them.

Piwo (beer) was virtually a national drink and a near necessity for working in the grueling conditions of the plant. There were occasions in the worst of the summer when workers actually died from the intense heat. It became routine for workers to stop at the nearby bars on the way to work and drink as much as they could before going to the factory so they could stand the dreadful conditions in the plant. More trips to the bars were made at lunch and after work. The situation grew so serious that John and Horace Dodge occasionally brought barrels of beer into the plant. At least that kept the workers on the job.

That all ended on May 1, 1917, when Prohibition went into effect—theoretically.

In fact, while Michigan enacted Prohibition, Ohio, just sixty miles south of Hamtramck, did not. And in Ontario, Canada, just a mile across the Detroit River, companies still manufactured liquor, although the Canadian government outlawed its retail sale. In short, the spigot was still open, and it began to flow almost immediately, toted in hidden gas tanks and under false floors in cars. The situation would take a dramatic turn, however, by 1919 when three-fourths of the states had ratified the Eighteenth Amendment to the Constitution, prohibiting the manufacture and sale of alcoholic drinks. The Volstead Act gave the federal government the means to enforce Prohibition, and on Jan. 16, 1920, America went dry.

It was a dark day, indeed.

In Hamtramck, Prohibition affected people differently. For some it was a welcome end to the bars that stole husbands and fathers away from their homes and drained their thin paychecks. But that view was in the minority.

For most it was at least an inconvenience. For others, it was life changing.

Such was the case for Joseph Chronowski. Chronowski came to Hamtramck in 1910 and established Auto City Brewing Company, one of a handful of breweries that would operate in Hamtramck. In the process he

Joseph Chronowski was a successful brewer who founded the Auto City Brewing Company in 1910 with his brother. When Prohibition hit, Joseph switched to the banking business, founding Liberty State Bank. But Auto City continued operating outside the law, until it was raided by federal agents.

acquired the financial skills that would allow him to make a complete career change when Prohibition came—he opened a bank. In fact, he opened it in what used to be the saloon he operated at Norwalk Street and Jos. Campau, which remains today in use as the Polish Art Center. The florid letters, "JC," are still highly visible, carved in stone above the front entrance.

Liberty State Bank was one of the more successful banks in Hamtramck. It weathered the Great Depression, partially because Chronowski used his own money to ensure that no depositors lost their savings. Chronowski didn't cut himself off entirely from the brewing business. Along with owning a brewery in Poland, he leased Auto City to a relative, who continued to brew beer in spite of Prohibition until he was arrested and sent to Leavenworth. Chronowski, however, wasn't implicated in the illegal operation.

Other brewers weren't as resourceful as Chronowski. Some, like Stroh's, switched to making nonalcoholic drinks, including orange soda and club soda or even ice cream. But many breweries simply closed, leaving their buildings boarded up and sold or left standing vacant.

National Prohibition and restrictions on alcohol imposed in Canada made it more difficult to get a drink and opened the way for the illegal liquor market.

Hamtramck was ripe for bootlegging. All the elements for a successful speakeasy subculture were in place. Alcohol was ingrained into the history and culture of the vast majority of the population, which was made up overwhelmingly of Poles. Much of the general population of America

After Prohibition, Auto City returned to legitimate business, tucked in the far south end of Hamtramck in the shadow of Dodge Main.

thought Prohibition was absurd. The Poles in Hamtramck, many of whom were new to America, likely were bewildered by this baffling law. They simply weren't going to stop drinking because of a law passed by who-knows-who for reasons as foreign to them as they were to the country. So if the bar was closed and you couldn't buy a bottle of beer or vodka at the store, you simply made it at home. And if you couldn't or didn't want to, there were plenty of people who would and sell it to you.

In short order, seemingly everyone was brewing and distilling, often literally in the bathtub. It was common for neighborhood kids to carry buckets of beer from the neighbors who produced the brew to their houses.

Speakeasies sprung up at a furious rate around the metro area. Fueling them was the position of Hamtramck itself. Completely surrounded by the city of Detroit, with just a small corner abutting Highland Park, Hamtramck was an island; significantly, an island with its own police department and political system entirely separate from the City of Detroit. For prominent Detroiters who didn't want to risk being seen in compromising places, Hamtramck offered a sanctuary outside the spotlight of the big city. The locals were more than willing to accommodate these guests.

Prior to and after Prohibition, bars and breweries flourished in Hamtramck. C&K Products opened in 1923 as a malt brewing plant. Malt was legal, and if you wished to turn that into beer, that was your business. After Prohibition, C&K became a regular brewery, but didn't fare so well and eventually closed in 1938.

It was inevitable that vice would flourish in the town. There was just too much money to be made, and conditions for making it were ideal. The tightly packed town offered a huge assortment of places for speakeasies, blind pigs and brothels to operate. From the outside, most looked no different from any other business or house. But inside, there might be a still set up in a bathtub or a tunnel in the basement connecting the building to an inconspicuous garage nearby where liquor was brought in without attracting notice. Within a few years, Hamtramck was a center of illegal activity to such an extent that it began to attract national attention.

"The Story of Hamtramck Where Detroiters Got their Booze and Night Life Thrills," was the title of a long article in the magazine *Follyology*, which labeled itself "A Digest of High Class Humor." But there was nothing funny in its story. "No hospital, no hotel, no railroad station! But on practically every corner and scattered between are saloons....Painted women, until recently, walked the streets and openly flaunted their tainted charms from undraped windows....Cafes and restaurants, thrown up like mushrooms in the hurried scramble for a location in this oasis, blazed all night with a life that has long ago disappeared from these United States."

Those words appeared in September 1924, and by then it was fairly routine for the Detroit newspaper to carry items about trouble in Hamtramck. "Federal Raids Result in Seizure of Liquor" related a January 2, 1924 article in the *Detroit Times*. It told of the arrest of Joseph Stafalso, whose house at 9130 Jos. Campau was raided and police found "a half-barrel of beer, a quart and a half of moonshine and 24 bottles of beer." But that was small stuff. On June 29, 1924, the *Times* carried a much longer story about a broader investigation involving fifty saloonkeepers operating in Hamtramck.

It's no surprise that about this time federal judge Arthur Tuttle quipped, "It's a wonder to me why, when you stop at a filling station in Hamtramck you don't get your tank filled with liquor."

At first, Prohibition violations were treated lightly by the courts; a first offense drew a $20 fine. After all, hoisting an illegal drink next to you might be a prominent politician or a lawmaker. If they didn't take Prohibition seriously, why should you? In fact, Prohibition violations were flagrant. Dodge Main workers could buy a shot of whiskey from cars parked in the lots nearby. In Detroit, the sale of illegal liquor was second only to the auto industry in generating revenue—$215 million—in 1929.

The lure of that kind of money was bound to attract more serious players. One of the first—and the worst—was Chester LeMare. He was one of the most vicious thugs ever to have anything to do with Hamtramck.

Beginning in the early 1920s, he operated the notorious Venice Café on Jos. Campau just north of Caniff. He used that as a base of operations to extort money from the brothels and blind pigs that flourished in town. He was so successful, he was known as the Vice King of Hamtramck. He had extensive mob ties that would serve him well even after federal officers would close down the Venice Café in 1922. LeMare was convicted of liquor law violations in 1926 but got off lightly when the judge upped a fine imposed on him and put him on probation. LeMare then fared quite well selling fruit to workers at the Ford Rouge plant as he ran the Westside mob. It all came to an end for him in February 1931, when he was shot in the head while in the kitchen of his Detroit home by someone he thought was a trusted associate.

During his relatively brief career in Hamtramck, LeMare did not operate a monopoly. Seemingly everybody was involved in vice in some form or another, including the city leaders. That was made most clear with the indictment of Mayor Peter C. Jezewski. This stemmed from what is one of the most notorious incidents in Hamtramck's history, when the state police seized a convoy of trucks carrying bootleg liquor into the city. The convoy was being led by Lieutenant John Ferguson of the Hamtramck Police Department. Ultimately, fifty-four people, including Jezewski, were convicted and sent to prison. This marked a disturbing trend among Hamtramck mayors—namely going to prison. Jezewski set the pattern, and several other city officials would spend time in prison before Hamtramck's wild days were done.

To the world outside its borders, Hamtramck seemed to be settling into chaos. For the average Hamtramckans, life went on as usual. They went to work, sent the kids to school and did the best they could to survive in a tough environment. That environment grew to include a staggering number of saloons and soda fountains—300 by some estimates—as well as blind pigs and brothels. In 1923, nine such "disorderly houses" were identified on Clay Street, between Jos. Campau and the railroad tracks a few blocks away. Most were small, offering the services of three to nine ladies. None of those establishments could compare to Paddy McGraw's place on the railroad tracks at Clay Street.

Patrick "Paddy" McGraw was a decidedly untypical Hamtramckan, yet his wonderfully colorful career may actually say a lot about Hamtramck's collective psyche at this time. Paddy McGraw was a criminal; he was also an admired and respected citizen who made many positive contributions to the community. The community was willing to overlook his nefarious activities, which in the big picture weren't all that bad. Given the notoriety and nature

Patrick J. "Paddy" McGraw was
one of the most colorful figures in
Hamtramck's history. His brothel on
the south side of town was legendary
in its day, drawing customers from
as far as Port Huron who would hop
on a train that conveniently passed
his front door. Among his many civic
activities, Paddy sponsored a baseball
team.

of his business, it would have been impossible for the police and politicians, as well as everyone else in town, not to have known what was going on there. In fact, Paddy's place was raided a few times and closed for a year by federal judge Charles C. Simmons. But it reopened. It was tolerated, at least by most people, and Paddy became somewhat of a local celebrity.

He came to Hamtramck in 1924 shortly after being discharged from the navy and opened his boarding house and saloon, Prohibition notwithstanding. Conveniently located on the railroad tracks at the far south end of town, his establishment was able to attract customers from Toledo to Port Huron who made the quick train ride to and from Hamtramck. Saturday nights were legendary for the action that took place at Paddy McGraw's. He had taken a cue from the Dodge Brothers and adapted the assembly line for his own use. The guys waited their turn as they progressed up the winding stairs to a lobby area and the series of small rooms where the ladies—as many as thirty-six—were waiting.

McGraw expanded his presence in Hamtramck in more socially acceptable ways. He was a member of the Hamtramck Indians, which had formed in the 1890s as the first social organization to operate in the city. He was a founder and member of the Hamtramck Goodfellow Newsboys, which sold newspapers to raise money for needy children at Christmas. He sponsored an amateur baseball team, the McGraw Tigers. An animal lover, he maintained a zoo behind his building where he had two bears, two monkeys, some rabbits and other small animals. He was known for taking in strays and caring well for them. He kept two large dogs tied to the bar, just in case, but rarely was there any serious trouble, although in one instance he and all his patrons were stripped of their money during a robbery.

Big and burly, McGraw was as contradictory as the attitude toward him. He was known as "hard-fisted but soft hearted," always ready to help someone in need and had a soft spot for the poor.

That likely contributed to the long tenure of his business despite the law. But it didn't protect him from the end of Prohibition. Located not far from Dodge Main, in an area littered with a host of other brothels, bars sprang up in his neighborhood when they became legal in 1933—the same year Paddy McGraw decided to retire. He closed up shop, sending the girls God knows where, and retired to his cottage at St. Clair, Michigan, where he lived quietly until his death on June 27, 1936.

There even was controversy in the circumstances of his death. One report had it that he was injured in an accident while working on his cottage. But police were also investigating a claim that he had died of injures when struck by a chair wielded by John "Sailor Jack" Gillis, a neighbor of McGraw's. However, the St. Clair prosecuting attorney dropped the investigation when an autopsy showed that McGraw had died of a heart ailment. He was sixty years old. A week later, the Hamtramck Common Council unanimously passed a resolution mourning his death. It read, in part, "Patrick J. McGraw was known from coast to coast for his philanthropic endeavors, and was loved, honored and respected by all who knew him....The members of this Council realize the great loss to this Community due to the death of our beloved citizen."

On the tenth anniversary of his death, in June 1946, the Hamtramck *Citizen* newspaper ran a memorial story reminding the community of what a great guy he had been.

The final eulogy for Paddy McGraw came in 1981 when the hulk of what had been his notorious business was destined for demolition. It stood at the edge of

Long abandoned, Paddy McGraw's brothel stood vacant for decades before it was demolished in 1981 as part of the redevelopment of the area for the General Motors Detroit-Hamtramck Assembly Plant.

the site of where the new General Motors Detroit-Hamtramck Assembly Plant was going to be built. By then, Paddy McGraw's building had been crumbling for decades and almost nothing remained to indicate its former glory.

On a drizzly, gray Saturday in September 1981, the building was demolished, and the rubble hauled away. A few remembered it and him, and some mourned the final passing of one of the most colorful pieces of Hamtramck's history.

Paddy McGraw found success during Prohibition as Hamtramck's rapidly growing reputation as a wide-open city was drawing greater attention, and the heat on the city officials was slowly rising. Even the *Dziennik Polski* (*Polish Daily News*) and the *Polish Record*, both prominent Polish-language newspapers, were taking note, running stories on the town's rampant vice.

In the midst of this, Hamtramck officially became a city in April of 1922, and Peter P. Jezewski was elected mayor. The Poles at last were beginning to flex their political muscle in a major way, starting the process to wrest power form the Southenders, the old-line, mainly German population that lived on the south side of town in favor of the Northenders, the new immigrant Poles who settled north of Holbrook Avenue. Although the first city council was made up predominantly of non-Poles, including Dr. James Henderson, an African American, future mayor Stephen Majewski was elected justice of the peace and fellow Poles Sixtus Janc and Casimir Plagens along with John Bucsko, a Ukrainian, were elected to the council.

Peter C. Jezewski was elected
Hamtramck's first mayor in
1922. And he was the first one
to run afoul of the law when
he was implicated in protecting
vice in the city.

But Jezewski was the key player. Originally from Buffalo, New York, he was
a pharmacist who set up shop at the corner of Jos. Campau and Belmont. His
pharmacy was a landmark for decades, noted for the glass globes of colored
water in the front windows and the live leaches he sold. At the back of the
pharmacy was an office area that Jezewski used as his political headquarters.

"He was the hub" of the Polish political movement, Majewski recalled
many years later. "Jezewski was a good man. He was a friendly man, but he
wasn't suited for the office of the mayor because he let things go. He didn't
have a firm grasp on the affairs of the city."

Indeed, the situation was growing worse even as he took office.

In September 1923, not long after the first common council was
established, it passed a resolution demanding that the administration clean
up the city. Introduced by council president John Bucsko and Councilman
Casimir Plagens and supported unanimously by the council, the resolution
demanded the mayor and police commissioner "perform their duties as
such and eliminate all disorderly houses from the city; that gambling be

Hamtramck Police carted many a lawbreaker in their paddy wagons. The vehicles were readily available—they were made in town at the Dodge Main factory.

stopped; that places which have been denied licenses be put out of business at once, and that transient merchants be stopped from selling their wares and merchandise in public streets."

The council threatened to ask for assistance from Governor Alex Groesbeck if action wasn't taken within two weeks to clean up the town.

The resolution was passed two weeks after the council approved a similar resolution that went so far as to require that each police office be personally "responsible for conditions" that exist on his beat. That resolution was placed in a gold frame and hung in the police station—where it was ignored.

In the second resolution, the council went on record raising the issue of bribery, noting the tolerance of the conditions by city officials "would not at least imply a reception of benefits from places which are not permitted in any other law-abiding community."

The council railed against the "deplorable conditions that existed in the city of Hamtramck in regard to the number of disorderly houses" allowed in the city.

"It would appear that these places must have some hold either upon the police department or upon those who have the appointment of the said department which prevents the taking of proper action against them....It

Hamtramck's finest—well, some were. But some of the police officers supplemented their income with bribes and kickbacks.

is evident that the officials of the city of Hamtramck in whom the power is vested by the charter and by the laws of the state of Michigan to enforce the law, tolerate these conditions to exist in the city."

The resolution was read into the record at the council meeting with no discussion. Mayor Jezewski and police chief Max Wosinski were in the audience but said nothing as well. After the meeting, however, Wosinski said he didn't see the need to respond to "every fool resolution" passed by the council. It was not an encouraging response.

And it got worse.

Within days of the council's resolution, Mayor Jezewski had fired up the political machine and the Polish American Political Club of Hamtramck threatened the entire council with a recall.

The club defended Mayor Jezewski, saying he "does everything possible to eradicate undesirable elements seeking refuge in our city." Further, the club claimed that Hamtramck was cleaner than any other city of its size in America, and that the charges leveled by the council were affecting property values by portraying Hamtramck as an undesirable place to live.

"We are advising the city council for the last time to stop playing on our nerves; to stop degrading us in the eyes of our neighbors with resolutions of this kind, to give the city better protection through wise and proper ordinances. If you do not heed this advice, gentlemen, we are going to start recall proceedings," the club stated in a letter signed by club officers Cass Zarzykn, a real-estate salesman; Alex Sledzinski, a factory worker; and Stanley Jablonski, an undertaker. The president of the club was street commissioner Stanley Dzwonkiewicz, and the club secretary, tellingly, was George Kosmoski, secretary to Mayor Jezewski.

The club went on to say:

> We positively know that the conditions in the city of Hamtramck, a city of over 70,000 inhabitants [actually at this time it was about 50,000] inhabitants, are far better than in any city of its size in the whole United states of America, and even in the world....We know, after investigation, that the police force now in the city of Hamtramck is numerically inadequate to cope with different problems arising in a city of such proportions as ours. We know that advertising our city as a place in which houses of ill repute and all kinds of vice is rampant, does not only hurt the reputation of the community, but also brings with it the depreciation of properties in our city.

The club was particularly upset with the fact that the council's resolution was published in Detroit's daily newspapers. Hamtramck was already becoming fodder for Detroit's press, which feasted on the city's continuing troubles. In that respect, they had a legitimate concern. But most of their other accusations were absurd, and, ultimately, it was Jezewski who would have the hardest time holding onto his seat.

The council did manage to get some action from the police, who upped the number of raids they conducted, in one case not only arresting everyone in a blind pig but also destroying all the furniture in the place.

But conditions continued to get worse. With no real improvements taking place, Wayne County prosecutor Paul Voorhies called for the Michigan State Police to take over police operations in Hamtramck. Governor Groesbeck complied with Voorhies's request. Between December 15, 1923, and March 15, 1924, the state police conducted 275 raids on "vice resorts." Sixty of these were raided a second time.

It was during this period that Governor Groesbeck threatened to have Mayor Jezewski removed from office unless there was a substantial improvement in town. In fact, he conducted a hearing to consider Jezewski's removal before abruptly ending it and giving Jezewski ninety days to clean up the city in March 1924.

Jezewski successfully ran for office again in 1924 and strengthened his position with a council that was almost entirely Polish, including Andrew Wisniewski, Max Wosinski, Sixtus Janc and Joseph Skomski. Dan Minock was the sole non-Pole on the council. They were strong supporters of Jezewski, but the mayor's troubles were far from over.

It isn't clear just how deeply he was involved in the illegal affairs that seemed so rampant. Jezewski, in trying to please the various political factions had managed to alienate many through his appointments, dismissals of appointees and feuds with powerful political figures, like Dr. T.T. Dysarz, who was somewhat of a kingmaker, and council president Bucsko. Jezewski also exercised bad judgment in the company he kept. He was known to eat at Chester LeMare's Venice Café against the advice of Majewski, who warned him of the dangers of being snagged in one of the many raids of the place. A particularly ugly event occurred during Jezewski's second term when someone robbed the Bank of Hamtramck, just across the street from the Hamtramck city offices on Grayling Street. In making his escape, the robber shot and killed a police officer.

Instead of "grabbing the reins" and appointing someone who would take charge of the police department, Jezewski let the situation ride. His police commissioner, Max Wosinski, who also was later convicted of vice charges, wasn't up to the task of cleaning up the town. This reinforced the public perception that anarchy ruled in Hamtramck and drew state attention to the city.

In another incident, a drunken police lieutenant tried to stage a one-man raid at LaMare's restaurant. He was promptly disarmed and beat up by the LaMare's men. Adding to the outrage, the men brought the officer's gun and handcuffs to the police station and gave them to the police.

Jezewski's troubles culminated with his indictment and conviction in the illegal liquor convoy incident. Even as he faced a two-year term in Leavenworth, Jezewski ran again for office in 1926, but was defeated by Majewski. Jezewski had appealed his conviction and then asked the governor for a pardon, to no avail.

Majewski described the city as "in turmoil." But what could he do? Jezewski was still popular with his supporters, but he could not be a viable candidate.

Almost by default, since no other members of his political circle wanted to run for office, Majewski entered the race and won. But he had little hope of making any substantive changes to clean up the town—the entire council opposed him.

With most elected officials serving two-year terms (in office, not jail), Hamtramck's political cycle moved rapidly. Things neither improved nor seemed to worsen during Majewski's term, but stagnation was not acceptable to the people, and Jezewski's still-loyal supporters were looking for a new candidate. From Leavenworth Prison, Jezewski gave his blessings to Dr. Rudolph G. Tenerowicz. Tenerowicz would become one of Hamtramck's most flamboyant political figures. The chief of surgery at St. Francis Hospital, which had been built in Hamtramck in 1927, Tenerowicz maintained an office on Jos. Campau at Holbrook Avenue. A thoroughly engaging person, he had won wide recognition across the community through his practice and for often providing free care to the poor.

Tenerowicz was elected mayor in 1928, and within months came under fire for not bringing improvements to the city's continuing woes. In June, 1928, Wayne County prosecuting attorney Robert M. Toms sent Tenerowicz a letter demanding that he take action to clean up the city at once or he would call in state and county police agencies to do the job. He particularly cited the number of houses of prostitution in the city.

Toms wrote to the mayor, saying:

> To my knowledge, there are at least nine houses of prostitution running openly, each house having from three to seven girls. On several occasions I have conferred with the authorities of your city, calling their attention to this condition and advising them the proper method of a successful prosecution of the operations and inmates. My suggestions, however, have only been partially complied with, and no substantial results have been obtained.... Prostitutes are released illegally almost as soon as they are arrested. No effort is made to prosecute the operators of these resorts or even to obtain evidence against them in spite of elaborate instructions on my part as to how to secure and present such proof.

Toms accused the Hamtramck police of making "idle gestures" to curb prostitution. He demanded to see "concrete results" that the police were making progress cleaning up the city, or he would call in other agencies to do the job.

In response, Tenerowicz issued an order to the police department demanding a crackdown on illegal activities in the city. He ordered Andrew Wisniewski, commissioner of public safety, to supply him with detailed weekly reports of the police department's activities. Police captain Joseph Rupinski was given the full-time job of closing down the brothels, although he quickly reported to the mayor that a sweep of all the ill-fame houses in the city showed no illegal activity.

"The girls have all fled the city," Rupinski said.

Dozens of brothels dotted Hamtramck. Only one of the original buildings remains. It still stands on Jos. Campau at the city's northern border with Detroit.

Perhaps they had. Toms told Tenerowicz that Detroit had cracked down on prostitution, and many of the girls there had fled town. Perhaps the Hamtramck girls had done the same; perhaps not. In any case, Tenerowicz said that any police officer found in a saloon or blind pig would face suspension or be fired.

We will not tolerate any such conduct on the part of our officers. For several weeks I have received complaints concerning individual members of the department. These will be thoroughly investigated and if charges are filed, any men found guilty will be immediately discharged. The police department will be completely reformed and changed, if necessary. Additional raids are being planned against all forms of lawlessness and there will be no letup until the city has become cleaned more than ever in its history. As long as I am mayor of this city, I hope to maintain such a program.

That was not likely.

While the remainder of Teneriowicz's first term was free of corruption charges, there is no indication that things had improved in Hamtramck. Prohibition was still fueling the local underworld, and after 1929, things took a dramatic turn for the worse with the coming of the Great Depression. Unemployment skyrocketed, and demands for relief soon overwhelmed what resources the city did have. People turned to the churches and organizations like Tau Beta and the St. Anne's Community House for support. They, in fact, had been a counterbalance to the evils that flourished during the Prohibition. They offered a range of social services as well as recreational opportunities. Because Hamtramck had grown so large, so fast, virtually no consideration was given to having recreational facilities in the city as it developed. Kids, for the most part, played in the streets and empty lots. As early as 1923, Stanley Jankowski, Hamtramck's commissioner for public welfare, criticized the city for not adopting a recreational program.

"Instead of starting at the root and building clean morals for your young people, the future generation, you do not give them recreation but leave them to find recreation in saloons and places of vice," he told the council, which did nothing. Two years later, in February 1925, the public schools took on the responsibility with the establishment of the Department of Recreation.

The churches and social organizations did what they could to provide aid to the needy and give some moral direction. Dances were common, held virtually every weekend at Kanas Hall, the Tau Beta Community House or at any of the many other halls across the city. They were wholesome outlets that reminded everyone that the rampant vice did not honestly reflect the true nature of the city, which was that of a hard-working town.

There seemed to be an inexhaustible supply of money to power the saloons and brothels, despite the economic woes of the Great Depression. In 1931, after Tenerowicz had won a second term, he was indicted by a Wayne County grand jury along with police chief Harry Wermuskerken, Councilmen Fred Dibble and Joseph Skomski, police captain Rupinski (who somehow failed to find the loose ladies in town) and Joseph Kaplan, head of another vice ring. All were charged with accepting payoff money from the various illegal sites in town to protect them.

They went to trial in January 1932 and heard a parade of witnesses outline how they had seen Kaplan collect money to distribute to the others indicted. Ultimately, charges against Dibble and Skomski were dropped, but Tenerowicz, Kaplan, Rupinski and Wermuskerken were found guilty, and sentences of between three and a half to five years were imposed. However,

You don't have to speak Polish to get the meaning of this cartoon that appeared in the *Dziennik Polski* (*Polish Daily News*) in 1923. The people of Hamtramck are being ravaged while the police and officials quarrel over the spoils.

they remained free on bail for nearly two years while the verdict was appealed all the way to the Michigan Supreme Court. Justices upheld the lower court's ruling, and the defendants were shipped off to prison. For Tenerowicz, that was barely a blip in his career because he would go on to be elected mayor again and then to U.S. Congress. Doc Ten, as he was popularly known in town, was so popular that a petition drive was soon organized to have him set free. More than 15,000 Hamtramckans signed the petition, which was presented to Governor William Comstock.

Comstock, a Democrat, surely noted the voting block those signatures represented and pardoned Tenerowicz eight months after he had entered prison. His official reason for the pardon was that Tenerowicz had been a victim of "political revenge." Within a matter of hours, Tenerowicz was back in his home on Trowbridge Street. At 9 p.m., two hours after he arrived home in December 1934, Tenerowicz issued this statement: "Naturally I am greatly pleased at having received a complete pardon from Governor Comstrock. It would be useless for me to even attempt to express my gratitude toward him. However, the past is past. It's better to try and forget it. From now on, I hope to spend my time in starting over again, in rebuilding my medical and surgical practice."

Fifty people were waiting for Tenerowicz when he returned home, and he spent the evening sharing beer and sandwiches with the well-wishers.

Somehow the beer seemed appropriate. After all, that primarily was what had got him into trouble in the first place. And there was an irony in that by the time his problems with the law were over, beer was again legal. On May 11, 1933, Prohibition officially ended, and the beer spigots were opened. Prohibition had been a national failure, universally ignored and actually counterproductive. As Mayor Majewski later put it, "it made law violators out of ordinary people that otherwise were law abiding."

The extent of Hamtramckans' thirst was shown by the sales at the State Liquor store in town. On the Saturday before Easter in April 1935, the store recorded the third-highest liquor sales in the state—more than $4,000. But even that did not match the New Year's Eve sales of 1934 when the store recorded $6,700 in sales.

The end of Prohibition did not stop bootlegging or any of the other vices that had become ingrained into the fabric of Hamtramck by that time. Moonshine stills were pumping out cheap—and sometime poisonous— bathtub gin in bathrooms, back rooms and sheds all over town. This was despite that fact that an enormous number of licensed bars opened in Hamtramck. It's difficult to estimate the exact number of bars operating at a given time because so many changed ownership over the years. It's been estimated that there were at least 200 bars operating at one time following Prohibition in its mere 2.1 square miles. They were virtually on every other street corner. Supposedly, Hamtramck had more bars per capita than any other city in America. Most were shot-and-a-beer places, often with no more than a row of seats at the bar. It was a place to get an E&B or Stroh's and a shot of Kessler's. Only one of those places rose to the status of a real night spot. The Bowery Nite Club stood on Jos. Campau next to the Woody Pontiac car dealership and, through the 1940s and early 1950s, drew many of the top entertainers in the country, like Sophie Tucker, Gypsy Rose Lee, the Three Stooges, Jimmy Durante and more.

At the other end of the spectrum were home breweries. Police uncovered a typical operation on Charest Street in August 1935. Acting on an anonymous tip, police found a twenty-five-gallon still with two gallons of moonshine

Bathtub gin remained popular long after Prohibition. This police raid occurred in the late 1940s.

and four barrels of mash. The still was not operating at the time of the raid, and no one was arrested. Three other men weren't as lucky in January 1936 when they were arrested and hauled into federal court for operating a still. And this sort of thing would go on for years after Prohibition ended. In the space of a week in September 1961, police broke up two separate moonshine operations. Two men were arrested when a police officer saw the offenders carrying buckets of booze out of a house on Dequindre Street.

Inside they confiscated a 280-gallon cooker, seventeen barrels of mash and assorted other equipment. A second operation was uncovered on the upper floor of a house on Dubois Street. Police had apparently just missed the moonshiners but did find fourteen 55-gallon barrels of mash brewing. They confiscated two cookers, fifteen 1-gallon jugs and other equipment.

These were small fry but typical of the type of vice that had become a part of the town's culture over the decades. Liquor wasn't the only source of problems. Gambling and prostitution remained issues for decades. In April 1940, police raided the Hamtramck Hotel, a "boarding house for girls," at 2110 Clay Street. Proprietor Mrs. Hattie Miller said she had been paying between $800 and $1,150 a month in protection money to the Wayne County sheriff and the prosecutor's office. In July of that year, Hamtramck police conducted a series of raids around town. Gambling paraphernalia were found at two locations on Jos. Campau Avenue and on Smith and Clay Streets. In the most dramatic raid, police smashed their way into the M. and

M. Club at 1906 Casmere at Dequindre Streets and arrested nine women and sixteen men for frequenting a blind pig. Liquor, dice tables and poker chips were confiscated. Later that day, several more places were raided.

Mutuel betting was another highly popular vice. Mutuels were a form of betting on horse races with the winnings coming for a pool of the total amount bet. Seemingly everyone got in the act with that one. Even *Time* magazine reported on perhaps the most unusual mutuel arrest in Hamtramck, in 1943. Police suspected a young couple of selling mutuel tickets. They frisked the man and wife and found nothing. Then they frisked their infant son and found sixty-three tickets in his diaper.

In February 1947, police chief John J. Wojciszak was put in a position of defending the city's attempts to wipe out vice.

"Hamtramck is a clean city," he said after police—with the aid of Wayne County officers—raided a mutuels operation in a candy store on Casmere Street. Wojciszak said that mutuels arrests were almost a daily occurrence in town as a result of the police department's diligence.

Mutuels were a low-level crime for the most part and didn't reach the level of Prohibition violations. But they were seemingly always around; likewise with the blind pigs. These were often set up in basements or backrooms of stores. Typical was the blind pig in the back of a florist shop at 3002 Carpenter Avenue, which was raided by police after officers stumbled across it on a Sunday morning. The owner, a forty-eight-year-old woman, and six men were arrested and four cases each of beer and whiskey were confiscated. Such raids would occur routinely from time to time over the years, pulling an assortment of people—men and women alike—into the courts.

Tom Ice, a retired Hamtramck policeman, pled guilty to operating a blind pig on Jos. Campau in October 1959. Because Ice knew everyone in the police department, a Wayne County Sheriff's Department officer was used to infiltrate the operation where he bought a bottle of beer for 30 cents and a pint of moonshine whiskey for $2 using marked money. Police confiscated $102.98 in cash along with $38.70 from a juke box, seven pints of whiskey, six bottles of wine, two gallons of moonshine whiskey, two pints of gin and several cases of beer.

By this time, the courts did not view these gambling operations with great seriousness—at least it appears that way with the sentences handed down to violators. Ice was ordered to pay thirty-five dollars to the Torch Drive, in lieu of a fine by Hamtramck municipal judge Rudolph Maras. The loiterers at the blind pig got off with orders to also make a twenty-five-dollar contribution to the Torch Drive.

The Berkshire Inn Motel and Robins Nest Restaurant opened in 1965 across from Dodge Main and was notorious for decades as brothel. It was demolished along with Dodge Main in 1981.

Less than a week later, five people were arrested at a brothel–blind pig on St. Aubin. Again, everyone hauled into court was ordered to contribute twenty-five dollars to the Torch Drive by Judge Maras.

Not as fortunate, however, was Peter Bielinski, who was wanted by federal authorities for operating a whiskey still in Hamtramck. Bielinski knew the feds were on his trail but he couldn't resist marching in the 1936 Memorial Day Parade, where he was promptly arrested by a federal agent—who wasn't fooled by Bielinski's fake mustache.

Well into the 1960s, blind pigs operated fairly openly in town. And even in the 1970s, a brothel operated on Jos. Campau near Casmere Street. And the Berkshire Inn, built in 1965 across from Dodge Main, was notorious until it was demolished along with the mighty plant in 1981.

But aside from the questionable use of video poker in some establishments into the twenty-first century, the vice of Hamtramck's wide-open years slowly withered and faded into another chapter of history.

CHAPTER 3
Their Wicked Ways

Starting in the 1940s, Hamtramck virtually renounced its wicked past. No one was interested in talking about it and local histories, such as the 1947 *Hamtramck Yearbook* printed on the twenty-fifth anniversary of Hamtramck's incorporation as a city. It carefully crafted a story that managed to avoid any mention of the city's turbulent past. Looking over the continuing stream of scandals, indictments, arrests and imprisonments that marked Hamtramck's early years, that's understandable. No one took pride in the string of mayors, council members, police chiefs and school board members who were sent to prison on corruption charges. The local and even national media had been brutal to the city, presenting lurid stories of gambling, prostitution, bribery, bootlegging and the occasional murder.

What's less clear is how that state of affairs came to be. How did intelligent, often well-educated, professional people get tangled into a vast web of corruption that at times seemed to stretch into every corner of city government and even the public school system? Prohibition certainly contributed to the rampant corruption. Prohibition was almost universally hated and felt by many to be an unjust law. Those who broke it—and they were legion—were not viewed by most people as criminals. The fact that many politicians and even police openly flaunted Prohibition and frequented speakeasies reinforced the sense that it was OK to break the law.

There was a lot of money to be made in bootlegging. Whether it was in producing liquor, transporting it or selling it to the public, money flowed like beer from a broken tap. The temptation was mighty—far too much for many to resist.

But Prohibition can't explain all the mischief. Long after Prohibition was repealed, vice flourished in Hamtramck.

Another factor that may have contributed to the lawless character was that too many people became accustomed to feeding off the public trough. For many years it was common for politicians to play musical chairs with the offices they held. Stephen Majewski, for example, at various times served as mayor, a school board trustee and justice of the peace. Vincent Sadlowski served on the school board and city council.

Joseph Lewandowski was mayor and served as justice of the peace. Constantine Cetlinsk served as a councilman, school board member and as city physician. Fred Dibble was on the village council and served as chief of police. Joseph Mitchell served as village clerk, city clerk, city councilman and city assessor. And so it went for many others, with a fairly narrow clique of political insiders not only holding elected offices but occupying appointed positions in between elections. This political inbreeding fostered the worst kind of familiarity as the politicians learned the system and manipulated it to their advantage with the assistance of fellow officials who were doing the same thing.

In some cases it was simple collusion, with those in power rewarding political supporters. But that shouldn't be taken to mean that there was one giant conspiracy of patronage. Indeed, the political groups were as fractured as a dropped mirror. Politicians often bitterly opposed each other even as they fed on the same system. Imagine lions, lambs and the occasional snake coming together for a moment of shared peace at the water hole.

Even so, the political scene became legendary for its raucousness, which included such infamous incidents as the occasion when a councilman pulled a gun on a mayor. The chaos lasted into the twenty-first century as council meetings commonly degenerated into screaming matches between feuding politicians.

Bad behavior seemed to be ingrained into the psyche of Hamtramck; perhaps it was.

Hamtramck's modern history began in 1910 when the Dodge Brothers came to town to build their factory. That prompted the explosive growth of the city, sending its population skyrocketing from 3,500 in 1910 to 48,000 in 1920 and ultimately to 56,000 by 1930. Hamtramck was the fastest-growing town in America. That is the key factor that distinguished Hamtramck from other cities. Most towns are established, grow and evolve over time. Some even die, but most follow a fairly straightforward path of development as they mature. Neighborhoods are defined, with industry

Two of Hamtramck's most controversial figures meet. On the right is Rudolph Tenerowicz. On the left is Walter Kanar, who succeeded Tenerowicz as mayor. Both men were embroiled in scandals.

segregated into certain areas, while other parcels are grouped for different types of residential, commercial and business uses. That's called zoning. But the concept barely existed in Hamtramck for decades as stores, bars, schools, houses and even heavy factories were crammed together often literally side-by-side. Such a mixture could often be found on the space of a single street in Hamtramck.

Vestiges of that can still be seen today. Hamtramck's neighborhoods were thrown up at a furious rate to take advantage of the immigrant influx. Houses were crowded onto lots 30-feet wide by 100-feet deep. That's too close to allow for driveways or even a decent degree of separation between neighbors. Such an arrangement would not be allowed in almost any city today. As the town bulged with people between 1910 and 1930, developers sought to maximize the useable land, and the early village administrators seemed unwilling or unable to exercise any type of control. So no parks were built; kids ended up playing in the streets and on dirty, empty lots; and rates of juvenile delinquency soared as kids formed gangs. When Prohibition came along, they were pulled into the cycle of vice that led from the streets to more serious crimes. Even after Prohibition, the kids were at risk. A stark example of that was the police raid of a pool hall in December 1936 at 1934 Caniff Avenue. Police had the place under surveillance for nine months, and when they finally did raid it they found forty gallons of moonshine hidden in a shed. The raid finally was conducted after two eleven-year-old girls were seen buying a pint of moonshine. At another time, a thirteen-year-old boy was seen buying mutuel betting tickets.

Hamtramck, like those kids, never had a chance to mature properly. The town went from infancy to adulthood in the space of a decade. The city suffered for it like a person who experiences a traumatic event early in life and never really gets over it.

Hamtramck was profoundly changed in the critical decade of 1910 to 1920. The rapid growth, nearly complete changeover of the population from Germans to Poles and the industrial development altered the nature of the town and set it on a unique path.

But why such a raucous one? It's tempting to say it is a reflection of the nature of Poles. They are tough and can be argumentative and stubborn.

Consider it was the vastly outgunned Poles who stood up first to oppose Adolf Hitler. Later it was the Poles who took the first steps to bring down the Soviet Union with the Solidarity movement. But they have also been quite willing to turn their wrath upon themselves. As early as the 1880s, Poles drew attention for their battles over the operation of St. Albertus Church in the Poletown region of Detroit, just south of Hamtramck. In that instance, two factions of the Polish parish were at odds, either supporting or opposing Pastor Dominik Kolasinski and the way he handled the church's finances. During the course of the conflict, parishioners literally battled in the streets, leading to the shooting death of one man. Years later, in Hamtramck, Poles fought Poles in a similar controversy with the pastor of St. Florian Parish, Father Bernard Zmijewski. On Sunday, March 14, 1909, a group of parishioners opposed to Father Zmijewski tried to block his entrance to the church, which had just opened (the parish was barely more than a year old at that time). Fighting broke out, and sheriff's deputies had to intervene. No one was killed, but one man was beaten with a club and another was stabbed in the hand.

It's interesting to note that in both cases this violence occurred in the shadow of the church—the most sacred spot in the community. But that obvious contradiction wasn't enough to cool anyone's temper.

For whatever reason, passions have always run high in Hamtramck. Sometimes that was most evident on the streets and not only in connection with the woes of the St. Florian Parish family. Nearby, but in a far different

Above: Not all kids were juvenile delinquents. As early as 1932, St. Florian School had a student safety patrol—a rather dapper one, at that.

Right: Mayor Joseph Lewandowski and his wife look over the shattered glass caused by a bomb that exploded near their bedroom window.

setting, someone blew up the White Star theater in March 1935. Theater owner M.A. Slepski said that enemies trying to put him out of business planted dynamite, which exploded and wrecked the front of the building, shattering windows a block away. No one was injured in the early morning blast, which police said was due to a labor dispute.

Another bomb blast drew far more attention a year later when someone blew up the garage by the Holbrook Avenue house of Mayor Joseph A. Lewandowski.

"Thousands are speculating over the exact motive for the crime that rocked Hamtramck," the *New Deal* newspaper reported. The blast occurred at about 11:35 p.m. on a cold Tuesday night. The bomb had been planted next to the Lewandowskis' garage. The blast knocked the garage off its foundation, blew the door to pieces and shattered the sidewalk. No one had been injured, but it could have been far worse. Lewandowski was at a campaign meeting with city attorney Thaddeus Machrowicz when the bomb went off, and his wife was at a card party at St. Anne's Community House. But their children Marcella, 10, and Jerome, 8, were asleep in the house along with a maid. The bomb blew up just twenty feet away from the bedroom window of the Lewandowskis' son. He was unhurt, but showered with glass. A neighbor, however, was cut by flying glass as she sat at a kitchen table. Windows at two houses on Lehman Street were also shattered. A major investigation was immediately launched with nearly every detective in the police department assigned to the case.

Four suspects were quickly picked up and quickly released on the strength of unshakeable alibis. Lewandowski put up a $500 reward for information leading to an arrest. An additional $500 reward was offered by Dr. Rudolph Tenerowicz, who was in a tough election race against the incumbent Lewandowski. Tenerowicz called the blast, "a most unfortunate incident."

The case took a bizarre twist when John Bendz, who had run unsuccessfully for the common council, told police more dynamite was being stored at a rooming house on Mitchell Street. Police found eight sticks of dynamite, a fuse and other paraphernalia under a back porch. But the woman who owned the rooming house was known to be a strong supporter of Lewandowski and said she knew nothing of the dynamite.

The bomb that blew up the Lewandowski garage was described by police as a tin can filled with gunpowder. But who planted it or why was never determined. It did, however, outrage Lewandowski's supporters, including the *New Deal* newspaper, which railed, "Their plot was the plot of a gangster. It was gangster in method and gangster in meaning. It was prompted from the same degrading impulses that left Leob and Leopold to kidnap and murder innocent Bobby Franks [referring to a highly publicized 'thrill killing' that shocked the nation]."

Whatever the motivation of the bomber was, the blast did nothing to help Lewandowski or hurt Tenerowicz in the election the following week. Tenerowicz won, 7,637 votes to Lewandowski's 6,476.

What happened next was a scandal of another sort. For once, ill-gotten money was not at the core of the story although that scenario was not foreign to Tenerowicz. He had already had served eight months in prison in 1934 before being pardoned for his involvement protecting vice operations in the city during an earlier term as mayor. That blot, however, had no impact on Tenerowicz's political popularity, as shown by his return to office. Rather, this was a story of human failings of the heart. Nevertheless, it scandalized and titillated the community in a way that maybe can't be appreciated today. Getting a divorce in the 1930s in a community as overwhelmingly

Mayor Rudolph Tenerowicz (seated) gets an absentee ballot from city clerk Al Zak in September 1942. A decade later, Zak would be elected mayor.

Catholic as Hamtramck was the stuff of hushed conversations. Add charges of adultery and the story became a shocker.

The first few months of the Tenerowicz administration were relatively peaceful, at least by Hamtramck standards. There were a few battles in the council chambers; the police fought for a pay increase; and the city asked the Wayne County Prosecutor's Office to investigate the possibility that the high cost of milk was being fixed by creameries. On the positive side, Dick Connell, director of public safety, reported that there was no evidence that the nefarious Black Legion, a terror organization akin to the Ku Klux Klan, was operating in Hamtramck.

The bomb (of another sort) dropped in July when Mayor Tenerowicz announced he was filing for divorce from his wife, Theresa. They had married in 1913 and separated in 1920. She lived in upscale Grosse Pointe Park, a world away from Hamtramck (even though that had been a part of Hamtramck Township until 1848) and, as far as the average Hamtramck was concerned, didn't exist. But she jumped onto the front pages of the local newspapers when she was sued for divorce by Tenerowicz.

In those days, divorce was a far more complicated affair, which could be contested by either party and dragged through the courts.

For once, the usually politically savvy Tenerowicz made a major blunder when he laid a series of charges against her, including that she was extremely jealous and meddled in his medical practice. But she seemed genuinely—and understandably—outraged when he accused her of being responsible for the deaths of their children through neglect by allowing them to be exposed to tuberculosis, from which she had suffered at one point in time.

In fact, their seven-year-old son, Rudolph, died of diphtheria; son Edward died of bronchial pneumonia at age two; and daughter Virginia died as a result of infantile paralysis. She said two of the children died at the home of her mother in Pittsburgh where she and the children were living while Dr. Tenerowicz was in the army during the Great War.

"The allegations that Mrs. Tenerowicz caused the death of her own children and the effects of such a charge on a good mother are pathetic," said her attorney Joseph P. Uvick. Mrs. Tenerowicz had wasted no time hiring an attorney to represent her interests, and she chose well. Uvick was a judge in Grosse Pointe.

Uvick said he would make no further statement. Dr. Tenerowicz said only, "I have not lived with my wife for 16 years. I have supported her all during that time. I might just as well be legally divorced now."

Those were just the opening shots.

Mayor Rudolph Tenerowicz's messy divorce made major headlines, with all the details played out in the newspapers.

Within a few weeks, Mrs. Tenerowicz filed a petition in circuit court seeking alimony of $290 a month. She said Dr. Tenerowicz's charges that she caused the deaths of their three children were so upsetting that she had to place herself in a doctor's care, increasing her living expenses. The court allowed her $190 a month, plus $12 for medical costs. Uvick pounced on the judgment, declaring that "Mrs. Tenerowicz will have to go to a rooming house. The mayor earns $18,000 a year." Dr. Tenerowicz was paid $5,000 a year as mayor; Uvick claimed he earned the rest through his medical practice.

In December the story took on the dimensions of a prime time soap opera when Mrs. Tenerowicz scandalized the community with her charges that Tenerowicz maintained two "love nests" in upper Michigan and was building a palatial $40,000 lakeside estate at Forestville, Michigan, for a third.

Further, she implied that Dr. Tenerowicz tapped city workers and equipment to build the estate. To add an extra sting to her charges, Mrs. Tenerowicz said the doctor's mother "has condemned the acts of her son repeatedly" and did not favor the divorce "because the Roman Catholic faith does not sanction divorce." But Mrs. Tenerowicz devoted particular attention to rebuffing the claims regarding the children. She said that he, as a surgeon, failed "to suggest that it was necessary for her to receive any treatment for tuberculosis or any other ailment." She added: "as a doctor he was the informant on the cause of death for the two children and furnished the history upon which the cause of death was in part predicated and he did not even mention tuberculosis as a possible cause and had not at any time suggested that defendant by her own neglect of conduct, caused the death of her own children, until, for want of better or real reasons, it became necessary to extricate himself from a legal God-sanctioned marriage to walk into the mire and depth of adultery and illegal co-habitation with one paramour after another."

Adding to the melodrama was that the three paramours were identified in court documents as Madam X, Madam Y and Madam Z. In Mrs. Tenerowicz's response to his demand for a divorce, Madam X was described as his main interest, always with him in his office and at the lake resort. "She publicly accused him in his presence of being the father of her child, the document stated. Madam X fell out of favor when Madam Y arrived on the scene. He often visited her, according to Mrs. Tenerowicz, and lived with her for a time at her lakeside cottage near Tea Lake in northern lower Michigan. She, in turn, was supplanted by Madam Z, whom "he has been keeping constant company, even since the filing of his bill of complaint, and that he has leased a summer home on the banks of Lake Huron and maintained Madam Z at the house and has spent many days and nights there with her."

Dr. Tenerowicz declined to respond immediately, but his lawyer, Herman August, said, "The doctor was threatened that her counter allegations would sizzle. So these charges do not surprise us. We deny the accusations and in due time will prove them untrue."

A few days later, Tenerowicz followed up with a formal statement:

> *All of the statements contained in the answer filed in my divorce have been inspired not by the desire of bringing out facts, but by my political enemies who have used my private affairs in the furtherance of their own political aspirations. I have definite information that an ex-official of the city of Hamtramck, still smarting from his defeat in the last election, furnished many of these false statements to the attorney on the other side.*
>
> *The entire answer was submitted to me before being given to the newspapers. I could have stopped its publication if I had been willing to pay certain parties a large sum of money. This I refused to do. This might not be blackmail, but it is so close to it is hard to differentiate.*

Their Wicked Ways

I promise the citizens of Hamtramck in a few days a true statement which will prove how malicious my enemies have been in circulating unfounded statements in regards to a summer cottage and these other falsehoods.

Shortly after making that statement, Dr. Tenerowicz appeared before a packed house in the common council chambers where he promised an investigation into the allegations that he built the love nest using the resources available to him as mayor.

"There are rumors around town about me building a certain cottage," he said. "I promise that I will myself get an architect and two house builders to go over the property and make a complete report right here in the council."

The building was a fairly imposing three-story structure with a long staircase leading to the shore of Lake Huron.

Whether he did bring in an architect and make a report isn't clear, for the case went silent for months. Ironically, the public attention was drawn away by another high-profile divorce case, that of Councilwoman Mary Zuk, who was best known for leading the 1935 meat strike and for the persistent accusations that she was a Communist. Her bitter divorce made the front pages of the local papers, but it usually was relegated to the lower portion of the pages. Dr. Tenerowicz's case was worthy of banner headlines.

"Seldom has any man received the notoriety for his love affairs that Dr. Tenerowicz has," the *New Deal* newspaper wrote in September 24, 1937. That was just below a two-deck banner headline: "Mayor's Wife Wins Cash and Alimony in Divorce." And below that was a large subhead: "Court Hears Love Affairs of Doctor."

The story related the end of court battle between the Tenerowiczs. Circuit court judge Lester Moll granted the divorce, giving the former Mrs. Tenerowicz a $3,300 cash settlement and $150 a month in alimony. Barely had the documents been signed when Dr. Tenerowicz announced he was going to marry Margaret McGuire, who had been identified as the paramour associated with the Forestville residence. Although not familiar to Hamtramckans, Margaret McGuire was known in Detroit social circles through her volunteer work with Eloise Hospital, her association with the Democratic Party and for serving on the state prison reform commission. He had met her when she worked with the Detroit Department of Welfare.

Within days of receiving the divorce, Dr. Tenerowicz and Ms. McGuire made a quick trip to Bowling Green, Ohio, where they were married to avoid a then Michigan law that required a certain period of time between a wedding announcement and the event. They returned to Hamtramck

This cottage near Forestville, Michigan, was identified as Mayor Tenerowicz's love nest.

briefly and then left for New York, from where they set off on a monthlong honeymoon exploring the Caribbean Sea.

In reporting the wedding, the *New Deal* newspaper concluded with a telling paragraph: "But of one thing all seemed sure—that Dr. Tenerowicz had married a very charming and disarming woman, one with whom he probably would be happy for the rest of his life."

Not only was the prophecy accurate, it demonstrated the immediate embrace the community extended to her and the instant forgiveness Dr. Tenerowicz received after months of scandalous coverage.

Once again Dr. Tenerowicz had taken a potentially disastrous situation and turned it in his favor. When he had gotten out of prison in 1935 and rather than being ostracized for his conviction, a huge party was held in his honor at Kanas Hall. And he was even given a new 1935 Chrysler as a gift by a group of local organizations including the Ladies Civic League.

In fact, Dr. Tenerowicz remained so popular that he was elected to Congress in 1938, crushing Republican opponent Charles Roxborough by a margin of 71,113 to 16,840 votes garnered across the congressional district.

But Tenerowicz wasn't invincible. After serving two terms in Congress, he was defeated in a bid for re-election in 1942 by his congressional successor, George Sadowski. Tenerowicz had lost the support of labor for his opposition to the lend-lease program designed to aid the allies opposing Germany in World War II. Feelings deteriorated so severely that in March 1940, a "bomb" was sent to Tenerowicz's Washington, D.C., office. It was no more than an alarm clock in a box, but the sender was listed as the CIO (Congress of Industrial Organizations), the labor organization.

In a crowded primary field, Tenerowicz drew a respectable 2,564 votes to Sadowski's 3,414 votes. But it was Sadowski who would go on to victory, representing the Democratic Party in November 1943.

"My sincere thanks to my many friends," Tenerowicz said in response to the loss. "My successor enters Congress when this nation and Democracy face their greatest test."

Dr. Tenerowicz indicated he was through with politics and would devote his attention to medicine. But he wasn't. He made another try for Congress in 1946 when he announced that he would run as a Republican—despite having campaigned earlier as being "fearless and liberal." But times had changed; he said the Democratic Party had betrayed Poland by allowing it to fall into the hands of the Communists following World War II.

"We must stop bolstering imperialism and Communism, and unless we cease our betrayal of small nations we are breeding a third World War....

We must start upholding free enterprise and Americanism," he said. While his message may have registered with the voters, his new political affiliation didn't. Hamtramck remained strongly Democratic, and Tenerowicz lost that year and lost again in subsequent tries for Congress in 1948, 1950, 1952 and 1954. Sometimes tenacity doesn't pay.

Dr. Tenerowicz died in 1963. It's difficult to evaluate his tenure as Hamtramck mayor. There were some significant accomplishments during his years in office, such as the building of Keyworth Stadium and the expansion of St. Francis Hospital, but that couldn't be directly attributed to him.

On the other hand, Tenerowicz held office through some of the worst years the city ever experienced, in Prohibition and the depths of the Great Depression—just surviving as a city was an accomplishment. Certainly his conviction of vice charges did not reflect well on the city or him. But, again, those were different times when flaunting Prohibition was an acceptable thing to do, regardless of the consequences.

But there's no question that he was one of the most popular and colorful figures in Hamtramck's history, despite his occasional bad behavior.

In that respect, Dr. Tenerowicz did not stand alone. Mayor Peter Jezewski also spent a year in Leavenworth Prison, and a host of political and police officials were indicted, with many convicted. Through the 1920s and 1930s, grand jury investigations of some sort of corruption or another were disturbingly routine events.

The culture of corruption peaked in the early 1940s with a pair of scandals that could not be passed off with a wink as the good old boys just being rowdy. Each alone was serious enough to cast a shadow over the city. But taken together, they represented a thoroughly disheartening picture that Hamtramck was corrupt across the spectrum. There was a near convergence of corruption as scandals rocked the city administration and the school system in quick order.

First, there's the city.

Walter Kanar was born in 1902 in Warsaw, Poland, and came to Detroit when he was about ten years old. He got into politics at a relatively young age and served as state representative in 1931–1932. And almost as soon as he was elected, he got into trouble. He was indicted by a federal grand jury on a charge of fraudulently obtaining his citizenship papers. The charge was eventually dropped, setting a pattern that would be a repeated in the future.

He was elected to the Hamtramck Common Council in 1934 and soon became embroiled in a serious controversy. In December 1934, Kanar and lobbyist Constantine Daniels were charged with attempting to bribe

Mayor Walter Kanar (left) confers with Fred Pabst, superintendent of the Department of Public Works, and Foss Baker.

state representative Michael Grajewski, offering to pay him $500 to try to block the recount of the votes cast for the secretary of state in the previous election. In a sworn statement, Grajewski said Kanar made him the offer in Grajewski's hotel room in Lansing. Kanar then left, saying he would return later. Grajewski immediately called the state attorney general's office. When Kanar returned, Judson E. Richardson, assistant attorney general, and another man were listening in an adjoining room. Supposedly, Kanar told Grajewski that "I can't get the jack together now," but that he was "going to see Teeny," an apparent reference to Daniels. He told Grajewski to call him the next day. In the morning, Grajewski called Kanar but got Daniels on the phone, who said he was sending Kanar over to see him.

Despite the seemingly solid case against Kanar, nothing would come of the incident. Kanar flatly denied that he was trying to bribe Grajewski and instead accused Grajewski of trying to bribe him. "Mike wanted me to fix it so that he would have not to pay back money he owes the city, but I refused," Kanar said. "It's just a frame up." Grajewski did indeed take money from the city from fees collected for the registration of birth and death certificates while he was city clerk. Grajewski defended himself, saying he believed that he was entitled to it.

This led to a separate investigation in the city, with the common council passing a resolution seeking restitution of the money. In any case, Kanar did spend the night in jail on the bribery charges, and the case was bound over to Lansing Municipal Court. After a couple of false starts, however, the case was dismissed in February 1935 after Grajewski consistently failed to show up for the trial.

The incident had no impact on Kanar's political career. He was re-elected to the common council in 1936 and 1938. But he was embroiled in controversy again in 1939 when Rudolph Tenerowicz was elected to Congress, and Kanar became entangled in a power struggle with Councilman Joseph Kuberacki to succeed Tenerowicz. For his part, Tenerowicz vowed not to leave the mayor's office until a successor had been named. For weeks the political factions battled as the story took a host of dizzying plot twists with Kanar and Kuberacki making peace, and Councilman Vincent Sadlowski automatically set in line to take over as mayor because he was council president. But at a Tuesday morning Committee of the Whole council meeting, Kanar got the council's support to be mayor.

That was reaffirmed at the regular council meeting later that evening as 1,000 people attempted to jam the council chambers. Kanar was in attendance, but declared himself to be "absent" and said nothing, merely watching the proceedings unfold. At the start of the meeting, Joseph Czarnecki, who was slated to become the next city attorney, said Sadlowski should excuse himself from voting because could not legally be the acting mayor and a councilman at the same time. Kanar was shrewd. He had formed an alliance with Councilmen Fred Pabst and Kuberacki and refrained from saying anything to circumvent an injunction being sought by Sadlowski to keep him from voting. With the vote split 2–2 with Sadlowski's vote challenged on sturdy legal grounds, Kanar basically assumed the position as mayor. He read a statement to the assembled crowd promising to prepare a plan to improve the city.

A colorful accent came in the form of seven baskets of flowers sent to the council chambers addressed to "Mayor Kanar." He had them sent to St. Francis Hospital.

Within a week, Kanar's presumptuousness was in fact supported by state attorney general Thomas Read, who affirmed that Kanar was legally elected as mayor. Kanar wasted no time in building his administration, firing four department heads almost immediately and replacing them with his own choices.

Twenty-four other firings or movements of personnel were quickly made. And almost just as quickly, the seeds of Kanar's downfall were sown. They came in the form of a new law authorizing the city to install parking meters along major streets in Hamtramck. In March 1939, the city received a bid to place 1,200 meters in the Hamtramck, although the council would ultimately settle on 500 meters from the Mark-Time Parking Meter Corporation of Detroit installed along Jos. Campau. Parking had always been a problem in Hamtramck, at least since the days when Dodge Main opened. Shoppers and residents alike have vied for the limited space available. This began to grow acute in the 1920s and especially the 1930s as the Jos. Campau shopping strip became the second-most popular shopping area in southeast Michigan, behind only downtown Detroit. With spots always at a premium, the city saw a viable way to raise revenue a penny and a nickel at a time through the meters. With acquisition and installation costs set at fifty-five dollars per meter, they could quickly pay for themselves and generate a handsome profit for the city.

It seemed like a good deal for the city, but three local businessmen sought an injunction in Wayne County Circuit Court seeking to prevent Hamtramck Ordinance No. 170, permitting parking meters in the city, from being enacted. Judge Homer Ferguson, who had presided over so many scandals in Hamtramck by this time must have known every nuance of the city, ruled that there was no reason to issue an injunction.

Nevertheless, as had become the custom so often in Hamtramck, the issue became the center of a controversy. An anonymous ad carried in the *New Deal* newspaper raised questions about the meters and Mark-Time. This prompted a full-page response in the *Citizen* newspaper, outlining "25 Reasons Why Hamtramck Officials Used Good Judgement [*sic*] In Selecting The MARK-TIME METER." The company defended the meters as "Compact and simple to operate"; Mark-Time's bid was the lowest received by the city; and the meters would be installed by the company at no cost to the city.

A story took a curious turn in the first week of April 1939, when Mayor Kanar sent a letter to the common council saying he was opposed to installing parking meters in the city. This was met with incredulity by the council members.

"His letter to the council dumbfounded me," said Councilman Vincent Sadlowski. "I cannot understand it. What's all the monkey business about?" He claimed he and Kanar had discussed parking meters before Kanar became mayor, and "he sold me on the idea that the meters were a good idea for the merchants and the citizens."

It was one of the new parking meters installed in the city, like this one, that lead to the downfall of Mayor Kanar.

"The mayor, if he were not in favor of the meters, should have put himself on record some time ago by vetoing the contract and ordinance," said Councilman Kuberacki. Councilman Sadlowski said the mayor had on two occasions told him that meters were good for Hamtramck. "If the mayor did not like meters and thought they were no good why did he sign the contract?" he asked.

Kanar said he didn't veto the measure because the council would have overridden his veto anyway.

Whether he was succumbing to pressure from some merchants who objected to the meters or was establishing an alibi will never be known. The parking meters, however, did go in and after some initial resistance—not to mention tampering with toothpicks and matchsticks—were accepted as part of the street scene. By May the first accounting was done, and it was found the meters had generated $252.27 in revenue. The top amount collected from one meter was $1.69 and the lowest was 2 cents. By June the monthly collection had reached $2,524.62.

As the revenue from the meters went up, the opposition seemed to go down as people got used to them.

But the meter was ticking on a scandal that would explode across Wayne County, from Grosse Pointe to Dearborn. In August 1941, a raft of more than twenty-five officials was indicted by Judge Homer Ferguson's grand jury on vice charges. Mixed into the bunch were former Hamtramck councilmen Kuberacki, Fred Pabst and Sadlowski. Kuberacki and Pabst were charged with taking $500 bribes and Sadlowski with accepting $1,200 for their votes to award the parking meter contract to Mark-Time; Mayor Kanar and his brother, Henry, were soon added to the list. Walter Kanar also was accused of protecting vice operations, and Henry was dragged into the affair for allegedly holding $11,000 for Walter Kanar in his safety deposit box. Former mayor Joseph Lewandowski also was indicted on charges of protecting vice operations, but was soon cleared. Councilmen George Banish and city clerk Frank Matulewicz were later accused to accepting $500 bribes from Mark-Time—an accusation that was confirmed by Robert X. Caldwell, secretary-treasurer of Mark-Time.

It was a mess. Just sorting through who was charged with what must have presented an awful challenge for Hamtramckans who watched the charges unfold. Even though Kanar had not been convicted of anything yet, the Wayne County prosecutor began proceedings to have him removed from office. In a trial before Probate judge Maurice Tripp, Prosecutor William Dowling declared he would prove there was a link between Kanar and vice operations in the city. But in early testimony, no direct link to Kanar was established. Hattie Miller, for example, operated a brothel in town and admitted to paying officials but didn't know where the money ultimately went.

The testimony was reviewed by Judge Tripp and then sent to Governor Murray D. Van Wagoner in October 1941 for a final decision on whether Kanar, as well as Councilman Banish, should be removed.

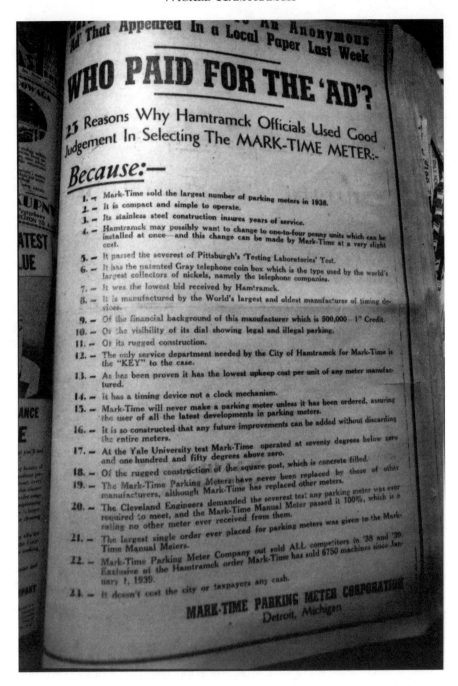

That Appeared In a Local Paper Last Week — An Anonymous Ad

WHO PAID FOR THE 'AD'?

23 Reasons Why Hamtramck Officials Used Good Judgement In Selecting The MARK-TIME METER:-

Because:—

1. — Mark-Time sold the largest number of parking meters in 1938.
2. — It is compact and simple to operate.
3. — Its stainless steel construction insures years of service.
4. — Hamtramck may possibly want to change to one-to-four penny units which can be installed at once—and this change can be made by Mark-Time at a very slight cost.
5. — It passed the severest of Pittsburgh's 'Testing Laboratories' Test.
6. — It has the patented Gray telephone coin box which is the type used by the world's largest collectors of nickels, namely the telephone companies.
7. — It was the lowest bid received by Hamtramck.
8. — It is manufactured by the World's largest and oldest manufacturer of timing devices.
9. — Of the financial background of this manufacturer which is 500,000—1" Credit.
10. — Of the visibility of its dial showing legal and illegal parking.
11. — Of its rugged construction.
12. — The only service department needed by the City of Hamtramck for Mark-Time is the "KEY" to the case.
13. — As has been proven it has the lowest upkeep cost per unit of any meter manufactured.
14. — It has a timing device not a clock mechanism.
15. — Mark-Time will never make a parking meter unless it has been ordered, assuring the user of all the latest developments in parking meters.
16. — It is so constructed that any future improvements can be added without discarding the entire meters.
17. — At the Yale University test Mark-Time operated at seventy degrees below zero and one hundred and fifty degrees above zero.
18. — Of the rugged construction of the square post, which is concrete filled.
19. — The Mark-Time Parking Meters have never been replaced by those of other manufacturers, although Mark-Time has replaced other meters.
20. — The Cleveland Engineers demanded the severest test any parking meter was ever required to meet, and the Mark-Time Manual Meter passed it 100%, which is a rating no other meter ever received from them.
21. — The largest single order ever placed for parking meters was given to the Mark-Time Manual Meters.
22. — Mark-Time Parking Meter Company out sold ALL competitors in '38 and '39. Exclusive of the Hamtramck order Mark-Time has sold 6750 machines since January 1, 1939.
23. — It doesn't cost the city or taxpayers any cash.

MARK-TIME PARKING METER CORPORATION
Detroit, Michigan

The Mark-Time Parking Meter Corporation was put on the defensive when a newspaper ad questioned why the city chose the company to supply meters for use on Jos. Campau. The company responded with its own ad.

For his part, Kanar said almost nothing. His only public comment as testimony was presented against him was that he "did not wish to dignify" the proceedings by responding to them.

Nothing happened, at least until January 1942, with the court testimony after it was sent to the governor until Van Wagoner reopened the case to hear new testimony from Kanar at the request of Kanar's attorneys William Fitzpatrick and P.J.M. Hally. This outraged Prosecutor Dowling, who accused Van Wagoner of "playing politics" and using stalling tactics to keep the hearing going until Kanar's term expired in April.

Days later, Kanar resigned.

Council president Anthony Tenerowicz, brother of Rudolph, assumed the office of mayor. Kanar said he resigned because Dowling was trying to use him as a "political springboard" to seek publicity in a planned bid to run for governor.

In any case, Kanar dropped from the political scene—indeed, he virtually vanished. He stuck to his word and did not seek re-election. Kanar ultimately was convicted of conspiracy to obstruct justice and was sentenced to a year in jail. He filed an appeal and remained free, eventually winning a new trial from the state supreme court in 1946 and obtaining an acquittal.

Even as the Kanar case played out, Hamtramck was rocked by another scandal on a different front: the public schools. And this, if not worse in scope, was far sadder, for it attacked one of the most proud accomplishments the city ever recorded.

In 1927, Hamtramck adopted a landmark school code that was so progressive it served as a model for school districts across that nation. It was so forward thinking that even today it reads as a modern document and is applicable to today's modern, technological, educational landscape. Hamtramckans took great pride in the school code, which was formulated by then superintendent Maurice Keyworth. However, after Keyworth left the district in 1935 to become state superintendent of public instruction, darker forces moved onto the school board. They saw a seat on the school board as an opportunity to pack their pockets with corrupt money by selling jobs. Simply put, if you were a teacher who wanted your contract renewed with the district, it would cost you $300.

The board maintained it had the right to dismiss any teacher it chose on economic grounds. But the school code gave the superintendent a great deal of power, including hiring and firing staff. That brought the superintendent in direct conflict with the board. To circumvent the code, the board decided that it had become obsolete by the summer of 1942 and no longer had a practical application.

That provoked outrage across the community. The *Citizen* newspaper of August 7, 1942, ran an obituary for "Hamtramck Education," complete with drawing of a cemetery monument on its front page.

"This is written in memory of a once-famous school system—the one that belonged to the people of Hamtramck....In recent years the greatness of the Code was forced to yield to an age-old enemy: Politics."

But it wasn't going to die quietly. Edward Barnard, attorney for the American Federation of Teachers, first aired charges of job selling at a school board meeting. This quickly caught the attention—once again—of the Wayne County Prosecutor's Office, which began an investigation. Simultaneously, the teachers' union had filed suit against the board on charges the board was practicing discrimination in renewing contracts based on Hamtramck residency, nationality or descent. These specifications, it was charged, were merely tools to use as leverage in selling jobs. In the course of the trial in circuit court, a host of allegations arose that the board was not only selling jobs but also engaging in outright theft of school property, including building material that ended up incorporated into the houses of some school board members.

As all this unfolded, circuit court judge Lila Neuenfelt signed a restraining order forbidding the scrapping of the school code. But this was not the end of the sordid mess. Months of virtual chaos ensued, marked by a two-day teacher strike, threats of recalls, protests by students and an outburst by school superintendent M.A. Kopka that was powerful enough to earn front-page headlines as he basically said he had had enough of the board's shenanigans.

Finally, the state had had enough as well. "A ray of hope that Hamtramck's school system may yet be salvaged from the depths to which it has sunk was given the citizens Monday night by Dr. Eugene B. Elliott, State Schools Superintendent," the *Citizen* newspaper reported in February 1943. After a two-hour meeting, the school board members allowed Kopka "full executive control" of the district's operations.

This did not end the school scandals. In 1946, another ugly incident grabbed headlines when four members of the school board were accused of corruption when a teacher attempted to bribe his way to a principal's position. While this became a distasteful topic around town, it ultimately went nowhere in the courts because the state attorney general and Wayne County prosecutor chose not to pursue it; there was more internal turmoil over the appointment of superintendents for the next two years.

But in 1948, Eldon C. Geyer was appointed superintendent. He had twenty-five years' experience in education and had served as superintendent in Port Austin and Battle Creek. With him came an era of peace in the Hamtramck public schools. By this point, the city government as well had moved away from its wild past. With the election of Dr. Stephen Skrzycki in 1942, the tide of corruption receded. While he couldn't eliminate vice, his ten years in office were scandal-free—a remarkable change from what had preceded him for decades. Early in his administration, the city passed Ordinance No. 196, which was "an ordinance to revise, consolidate, codify and add to the ordinances relating to the preservation of the public peace, morals, safety and welfare."

It covered a host of areas, including indecent and improper conduct, houses of ill fame and keeping or occupying a building for gambling. It's not that these sorts of things were legal prior to the law (although it might seem like they were), but the ordinance emphasized that the city had had enough. The people of Hamtramck were finally fed up with all the scandals, the corruption and the press that was so bad at one point the city became the butt of comedians' jokes.

The early 1940s brought another element to the scenario: World War II. Hamtramck was thrust into the war like no other city. Many Hamtramckans had close relatives living—and dying—in Poland, which was Hitler's first battlefield target. Thousands of Hamtramckans served in the war. When they came home, they wanted peace.

And Hamtramck was finally able to deliver it.

CHAPTER 4

She's a Commie!

The concept of Poles cozying up to Communists is curious. Consider that the Russian army, under the direction of Vladimir Lenin, clashed with the Polish army in 1919—not long after the Russian Revolution—over control of Ukraine. In fact, the Poles and Russians had a long history of animosity dating back centuries when Poland was carved up by the Germans, Russians and Austrians during the periodic wars that ravaged Europe.

During the reign of the czars, many Poles came to America specifically to avoid being drafted into the Russian army. Prior to World War I, Poland ceased to exist, but was re-established in the wake of the war. This was a short-lived situation that ended in September 1939, when the Germans— and two weeks later the Russians—invaded, igniting World War II. But in that brief period of independence, Poland was capable of standing up against the Soviets, who were still in turmoil in the wake of the revolution of October 1917.

Communism was not invented in Russia, of course, but the concept grained strength and an identity with the Bolsheviks.

Here, the Socialist Party of America, the father of Communism, was founded in 1901 in a reaction to the often-appalling conditions of the working class, which stood in sharp contrast to the upper class. The Russian Revolution did give a boost to the movement, which had never gained much momentum in America, at least not to the extent that it affected American policy or swayed many elections.

Still, the events in Russia were disquieting. Lenin had made it clear he believed in a violent worldwide revolution. And there was the disturbing fate of Czar Nicholas II and the royal family, who were unceremoniously shot in the basement of a remote house deep in the forests of Russia.

For a rich capitalist in America, that was troubling. They worked hard to paint the Socialists and more radical Communists as a threat to American society and who were dedicated to overthrowing the government. The attack, which was highly successful, served to alienate the Communists from the mainstream public. Sometimes, more than words were used. On January 2, 1920, an army of state police officers led by federal agents raided the dance hall on Gratiot Avenue and St. Aubin. Known as the House of the Masses, it had become a popular meeting place for the Socialists over the past two years. About 200 were arrested and hauled off to a makeshift jail at a post office. Three hundred others had already been arrested that night in Detroit. Similar raids were conducted in thirty-two other cities across the nation, where about 5,000 immigrants were rounded up to be deported as undesirable aliens. Little consideration was given to their rights as these new Americans were subjected to the most un-American treatment. Many were summarily deported without a hearing.

It was shabby treatment, but it was not unexpected. Standing up to the establishment has always had its risks. But many people saw it as the only way to improve their lives. That's what caused them, particularly laborers, to put aside whatever political, ethnic or social differences they had to embrace a common cause. Call it Socialism or Communism, it really didn't matter to the immigrant laborers who barely tolerated the typically awful working conditions in the factories. It was a dangerous environment where injuries were common and death not uncommon. It was unbearably hot in summer, noisy all the time and reeking with the fumes of paint and chemicals. If you were injured, you were on your own. Even those who held on to the jobs had to resort to extraordinary actions: the foremen expected gifts, and it was common for workers to spend time and effort doing jobs at the bosses' houses. The workers had no voice and risked being fired just for going to the bathroom.

If they didn't like it—tough. There was always plenty of other of people looking for jobs who would gladly take yours, miserable as it may have been. The poor working conditions and steadfast and often-violent resistance to any improvements by those in charge led to the creation of labor unions. The Socialists, and later the Communists, saw a natural connection to the goals of the unions. After all, both strove to improve the lives of the working class. Hamtramck had its own House of the Masses. The International Workers Home on Yemans Street was built in 1919 and served as a major hub of the area Communist Party for decades. Countless rallies, speeches and meetings were held in this hall, and through the years it came under the scrutiny of police and federal agents numerous times. We can only imagine today what nefarious plots were crafted in the fairly modest two-story brick structure. *The Good Neighbor* newspaper, printed by the City Communist Party, listed the hall as its business address. To satisfy the workers' hunger for food as well as social justice, a restaurant was established in the hall. However, in 1927, the Workmen's Cooperative Restaurant was established just down the street. Over the years it became familiarly known to the locals simply as Russians. Now known as Polonia restaurant, it has long since shed its Communist association; but a Depression-era photo of President Franklin D. Roosevelt still hangs on a wall.

Like most ethnic groups, the poor residents in this period tended to cling together, relying more on family, friends and the church rather than political organizations to help weather the trying times. But conditions in the factories only got worse. In good times, the pace of production was grueling as factories hustled to keep up with demand. Those who didn't lose their jobs during the Great Depression were faced with faster production lines to

The International Workers Home on Yemans Street was built in 1919 and served as the headquarters of the local Communists for decades.

make up for the reduced labor force. Strikes were often violently suppressed. Perhaps the most infamous example would occur in 1937 in the Battle of the Overpass at Henry Ford's Rouge plant.

On the morning of May 26, about sixty members of the United Auto Workers, led by Walter Reuther and Richard Frankensteen, went to the plant's main gate and walked onto the overpass at Miller Road. There they were set upon and badly beaten by thirty-five security officers from the plant. Because of an odd twist of circumstances, that event ended up having a direct connection to Hamtramck. Assault charges were brought against the Ford Motor Company and seven security officers, but they were dismissed by Wayne County circuit judge Lester S. Moll after the defendants were bound over for trial. In response, Prosecutor Duncan C. McCrea re-filed the charges in Hamtramck court, contending that any judge in Wayne County had jurisdiction to hear the case.

Larry Davidow, attorney for the UAW, was delighted to see the case shifted to Hamtramck, saying, "I am confident we will get a fair and square trial. I don't believe there will be any prejudice shown toward any of the parties concerned."

Oh, how wrong he was. The case became embroiled in controversy when Hamtramck judges Nicholas Gronkowski and Arthur Rooks made contradictory rulings over whether the Ford Motor Company could be charged with assault because it was a company, not an individual. As the two judges battled verbally, it was learned that Gronkowski had given five dollars to the UAW for an Organize Ford campaign. This drew charges of favoritism toward the UAW on Gronkowski's part. He denied that, but the matter was handed over to Wayne County circuit judge Homer Ferguson, who saw things otherwise, voiding a ruling by Gronkowski that Ford could be sued.

There's no indication that Communists played any direct role in the Battle of the Overpass, although they did become deeply involved in the UAW until they were essentially purged from the union in the late 1940s.

But twenty years earlier, they were finding growing support in Hamtramck, not for their political ideology but for the things that mattered at home. That concept was essential. There's no indication the Hamtramckans who supported the Communists—or more properly, the goals of the Communists—were interested in exporting world revolution. The hard-line Communists did, indeed, defend the policies of Lenin and even worse ones of Joseph Stalin. But those names meant little or nothing on the factory floor where the average worker was willing to grab onto any lifeline tossed to them, even if Stalin was at the other end.

She's a Commie!

The Communist Party election slate of 1934 features the party's perennial candidate for mayor, George Krystalsky. The Communists did not fare well politically, but they did bring social issues to the attention of the population.

79

Consider the Communist Manifesto of 1934, which outlines a series of demands including: a minimum of seventy-five cents per hour for all factory workers; immediate cash relief for all unemployed without any discrimination against African Americans or the foreign-born at a rate of ten dollars per week for each single person, fifteen dollars per week for each family of three and an additional two dollars per week for each dependant, pending the enactment of unemployment insurance paid by the employers and federal government for all unemployed workers; free, hot, nourishing lunches in the public schools; social insurance paid by industry and government covering sickness, occupational disease, accident, maternity, old age pension; no discrimination against African American workers; the right of workers to join the union of their choice; the abolition of inhuman speed-up systems on the belt, etc.; and it should be unlawful to discharge or refuse employment to any worker solely because he or she has reached the age of forty or more years.

There was more, but these give a sense of what was being promoted by the Communists. Not a hint of the joys of collectivism or world domination, but exactly the issues that would register with the factory workers.

Attached to the manifesto was a slate of candidates, including Cass Bailey, an African American, and Jeannie Romaniuk, a woman. Remember, this was 1934. Chief among the candidates was George Kristalsky, who officially was a section organizer for the Communist Party of America, a perennial candidate and prominent figure with the Hamtramck Communists. In the election of 1940, he ran for common council and garnered a respectable 1,372 votes, finishing sixteenth among forty-four candidates. But he was far from being the most successful Communist to run for office.

That honor belongs to Mary Zuk, the first women ever elected to the Hamtramck Common Council.

Or does it?

Zuk was always coy about her Communist ties, preferring to say that most workers in America were actually Communists. One short report in the *Citizen* newspaper in August 1936 quotes her as admitting to a crowd at a political rally that, "I'm a Communist, and proud of it." That seems rather out of character for her, however, and isn't verified by other sources.

Regardless, her story is one of the most fascinating in the history of Hamtramck.

Born Mary Stanceus in 1904 in Neffs, Ohio, her father worked in the mines. After he was killed in one, Mary moved to Detroit where she lived with a sister. When she was fourteen years old, she lied about her age and got

She's a Commie!

Mary Zuk established her reputation as a fighter for the people with the meat strike in 1935. She also was the first woman elected to the common council, despite charges that she was a Communist. *Courtesy of Walter P. Reuther Library, Wayne State University.*

a job in one of the factories. At age seventeen, in August 1922, she married Stanley Zuk. They moved to Hamtramck where she settled into the life of a housewife, having two children with Stanley by the time she launched her career in public life. Described as five feet tall with dark hair and dark eyes, she didn't fit the image of a rabble-rouser. What brought her to prominence was her association with the meat strike of 1935. It is one thing to abuse and take advantage of the ordinary laborer, but it's quite another to raise the wrath of mothers and wives struggling to feed their families, as the local butchers learned in the summer of that year. It was still the depths of the Great Depression when money was tight. An increase in the cost of meat prompted a group of Hamtramck women to take action. They formed the Women's Committee for Action Against the High Cost of Living. Zuk, who took an especially militant stance, soon emerged as leader of the group. They organized pickets in front of local meat markets, carrying signs that read, "Strike for 20% cut in illegal prices" and "Meat packers make millions."

The effort outraged local butchers. "The markets have no customers," said Walter Mendrzyk, president of the Hamtramck Butchers and Grocers Association, as he announced that the meat shops would close for two weeks in August. That did nothing to deter the strikers, and their pickets soon spread to meat shops in nearby Detroit. As the lines of the picketers swelled, it became apparent that this was more than just a group of irate mothers venting their frustration. The butchers responded that the price of hogs had been rising steadily since 1929, and they were merely passing along the climbing costs. Further, the drought in cattle country out west in what had become the Great Dust Bowl, compounded by government-mandated

Meat strikers rally in front of a restaurant in Hamtramck in August 1935. The strike soon spread across metro Detroit and even to other cities in the nation. *Courtesy of Walter P. Reuther Library, Wayne State University.*

slaughterhouse policies and taxes, forced a 25 percent increase in the price of meat. Meeting at the Polish American Century Club on Holbrook, the butchers organized their own committee to present their side of the story. "The strike is ruining us," Mendrzyk said. "We're not responsible for the higher meat prices and we didn't see any reason why we should be made to suffer. We were considering closing our stores entirely until the whole thing blew over but that would cause a heavy loss for us. So we decided to stay open and start a little campaign of our own."

It was a risky move, but understandable. During the week, most of the butchers had closed their doors and let their meat spoil in their ice lockers. They couldn't afford to sustain losses like that.

Three weeks after the strike had begun, it spread down Chene Street to the old Poletown neighborhood south of Hamtramck and across North Detroit. Soon mothers in communities as far away as Lincoln Park and Wyandotte vowed to boycott butcher shops there. Nationally, similar women's councils were being formed and organizing strikes in a host of cities, including Boston, Philadelphia, Kansas City, Denver and Miami.

In early August, Zuk led a parade of between 300 and 400 women down Jos. Campau. For the most part, the strikers were peaceful although generally raising a ruckus and irritating the local officials. And in that, they succeeded mightily.

While the city administration was mainly favorable to labor, these strikers drew a much harsher response, possibly because their effort hurt local businesses and brought a wealth of negative publicity to the city. Further, a Saturday protest turned violent, causing an estimated $65,000 in damages to local businesses.

"We are with you in your intentions of reducing the price of meat but when you go about it the way you did last Saturday, we want to have nothing to do with you," common council president George Banish said as he introduced a resolution condemning the strike.

"You accomplished only one thing," Councilman Constantine Cetlinski said. "You gave Hamtramck a black eye."

Mayor Joseph Lewandowski spoke in even sterner terms. "It will be just too bad for you if you attempt anything that is just a bit outside the law," he said. "You not only accomplished nothing with your methods but brought shame upon the city. Again I warn you that it will be just too bad if you start something. We'll know how to take care of you this time."

So did the butchers. They said they would take up their meat cleavers to protect their property.

Another element that didn't sit well with the politicians was the possible involvement of Communists in the strike. Mayor Lewandowski labeled the strikers as Reds, echoing a sentiment expressed by a number of other officials. Zuk, who came under withering criticism at a common council meeting, was accused of being a Communist—a charge she denied. That denial was addressed directly in a caption of Zuk's photo on the front page of the *New Deal* newspaper on August 2, 1935, during the height of the strike. With or without local support, the strikers vowed to press on, and Zuk carried the cause to Washington, D.C. A committee of women, led by Zuk, hoped to meet with President Franklin Roosevelt but only got as far as secretary of agriculture Henry Wallace. The women wanted lower meat prices and an investigation of the meat industry. What they got was the familiar explanation from Wallace that the price hike was caused by the drought, and there was a possibility of an investigation of the meatpackers' profits. Reportedly, Zuk said, "Aren't you going to give us a definite reply?"

as Wallace fled from the room after trying unsuccessfully to bar the press from witnessing the meeting.

The trip to Washington did little good and, in fact, drew national charges of Communist involvement against the strikers. Congressman Clarence Cannon, a Democrat from Missouri, introduced a resolution in the House demanding an investigation of who was financing the meat strike, inferring that it was backed by the Communists and saying the strike leaders were "foreigners and Communists." Zuk and the ladies invaded Cannon's office to protest what she called "unjust insinuations." By the time the women were done with him, he was calling "Wait! Wait!" after them as they stormed out. Congressman George Sadowski, a Democrat who represented the Hamtramck area, came to the defense of the women on the floor of the House, denouncing Cannon and pointing out that the strikers were not taking aim at the farmers who produced the meat but at the various middlemen who tacked their profits on to it as it made its way to the stores.

"I was deeply hurt to have these women referred to as foreigners and Communists," Sadlowski said in his speech on the House floor. "I resent very much having such remarks made about the people of my district. Some people would still label a man a foreigner even though he were a third or fourth generation American simply because he carries the name of his forefathers brought from Poland, Italy, Russia, Romania or Czechoslovakia."

A pair of resolutions was introduced in the House and Senate seeking an investigation into the meat producers and packers. The resolutions were approved but killed by a filibuster led by Senator Huey Long of Louisiana before the appropriations to enact the measure could be approved.

Zuk took a brave stance on returning from Washington, saying, "We will continue to picket this week as usual." But it was clear the battle was lost. "The strike is over as far as the butchers and grocers are concerned," Mendrzyk said. "Last week some of those who had picketed us in the first week came in to buy meat. In a short while when the young hogs are put on the market, there will be a natural reduction in the price of meat. Then the strikers will probably think that they have won a victory."

In fact, Kroger Co. did cut meat prices by 20 percent. But the strike was fading. Five week after it had begun, the butchers saw a steady increase in regular business, and the courts began issuing injunctions to stop the picketing.

If there was a winner in the strike, it was Zuk. The charges of being a Communist bounced off her with seemingly little effect. To many she was a hero, a voice for the oppressed. At the encouragement of Rudolph Tenerowicz, who had served two terms as mayor from 1928 to 1932 (and was eyeing another run for that office), Zuk entered the race for the common council. Her campaign focused on demands for reduced rents, utility and food prices—none of which were under the jurisdiction of the common council. And she emphasized the message that she was a mother, and mothers were a source of power, as was shown in the meat strike.

But the *New Deal* newspaper wasn't buying it. The paper managed to run two editorials pillorying the Communists without naming Zuk. "The Communists are 'backing' a candidate for the Common Council. By electing this candidate, they hope to fasten their evil claws into Hamtramck's city government….The voters of Hamtramck know that under Communism there are no families—that Communism takes the babies from the mother and father before they are weaned—that the mother and father do not see them again. The voters of Hamtramck will elect five able members Monday. They will say again to the Communist Party 'you cannot run our city. You can't trick us into supporting your godless party.'"

It was pretty heady stuff. Even so, Zuk eked a council win, coming in fifth with 5,832 votes. Surprisingly, the local press made little of the fact that Hamtramck had elected its first woman councilperson—who just might have been a Communist. Zuk, who was not at all shy, didn't hesitate to share her opinions and challenge others. In May 1936, shortly after taking office, she got into an altercation with the city's welfare director over services being provided by the city. A bigger blowout occurred in August 1936 when Zuk and council president George Banish got into a verbal brawl over the Spanish Civil War, which came up as part of a general discussion on Communism.

"Look at what the Communists are doing in Spain—killing helpless men, women and children, and burning churches. Do you think that's right?" Banish asked Zuk.

"The Fascists are responsible for a lot of that," Zuk replied.

"How about the Reds?" Banish pressed.

"Well, we'll have to go down into the detail of the Reds," she responded. "How do you know the reports we read in the paper are true?"

"What about Communists in this country?" Banish asked. "Do you think they are all right?"

"The Communists are nothing but the majority of the working people of this country," she shot back.

According to a report in the *Citizen* newspaper, after the meeting a reporter asked Zuk if she was a member of that majority. After making references to the Constitution of the United States, she replied, "I belong with the majority."

It got worse. In October 1936, Zuk held a meeting at Kanas Hall on Conant, advertised as "Labor candidate Mary Zuk's report on her work in the council." At the meeting, in which Communist literature was freely passed out, Zuk blasted her fellow council members for not approving a 20 percent raise for welfare recipients.

The following Tuesday's common council meeting took on overtones of the coming Second World War. Councilman Walter Kanar, furious, attacked Zuk. "The Zuk meeting was characterized by nothing but lies," he shouted. "Mary Zuk has not done one thing for the working man ever since she's been in office. The only thing she ever took credit for was the 5 percent raise in the pay of D.P.W. (Department of Public Works) workers. And then it was Councilman (Joseph) Kuberacki's resolution and my amendment that made this raise possible."

Kanar went on: "I wouldn't like to have you fight for me. I'd rather starve before you would do anything for the working man."

"I wouldn't fight for a prisoner," Zuk responded.

"That's enough, Communist," Kanar shouted.

Council president George Banish joined in the fray, saying the council had supported her resolution to approve a 20 percent welfare pay hike. Then Banish jumped on her about the Communist literature distributed at the meeting.

"Why should I stop the Communists? Haven't they just the same rights as you Republicans?" Zuk replied.

Councilman Kuberacki tried to bring some order to the meeting. "Can't we work together instead of fighting?" he implored.

Apparently they couldn't.

"Poor little Mary Zuk," Banish taunted, picking up the fight again. "There's four against me. What can I do?"

"We'll go to Washington to get what we want," Zuk replied.

"Those Communists are certainly educating you right," Banish shot back.

Zuk was unbowed. She continued her activities outside the council chambers, at one point being forced to jump from the second story of a factory where she was agitating.

However, her rapid downfall didn't result from charges of Communism or feuds in the council chambers. It was brought about by her divorce. In April 1937, word got out that Zuk had filed for divorce from her husband, Stanley. A month later, the divorce rated a banner headline in the *New Deal* newspaper. "She completely ignored me right after she was elected," Stanley Zuk told the paper. "She often went out in the evening and never came back until some time during the next day. She never told me where she spent the time."

She's a Commie!

In her divorce suit, Mary Zuk charged her husband with extreme cruelty, physical abuse, excessive drinking and failure to support her and their children. Stanley responded that she was a contributor to the Communist Party and neglected the children. The divorce was granted in September 1937. Mary Zuk got custody of the couple's two children and alimony of $2.50.

Interestingly, as this messy divorce was being played out in the pages of the newspapers, another high-profile divorce was grabbing even bigger headlines. Mayor Tenerowicz was going through an exceptionally tangled divorce from his wife. In fact, his divorce was far more lurid than the Zuks'. Tenerowicz had accused his former wife of being responsible for the deaths of their children years earlier. Several women came forward to say they had had affairs with him. Tenerowicz, however, had one advantage: he was a man, and his foibles would be excused. The predominantly Roman Catholic community that elected Zuk looked down on a divorced woman holding office.

In the primary election of March 1938, Zuk finished a distant eighth, even behind George Kristalsky, who garnered 300 more votes than she did. Her showing in the April general election was even worse. She finished tenth—last place—in the council race.

It wasn't quite the end of Zuk's public life. Within a few weeks Tenerowicz appointed her as the city's water inspector. But in November 1938, Tenerowicz resigned after being elected to Congress. Zuk managed to hang on to the position until the following March when her old nemesis, Walter Kanar, fired her.

Zuk slipped out of public life. In 1940, she married Joseph Varto, and they had a son. After that she lived quietly out of the public spotlight until her death in 1987.

The Communist movement in Hamtramck did not end with Mary Zuk. Thomas X. Dombrowski, a well-known Communist, ran for U.S. Congress in 1940 and twice for the Hamtramck Common Council. He is perhaps best known for editing the English section of the *Glos Ludowy* (the *People's Voice*.)

World War II brought a whole new aspect to Communism here. At first fiercely opposing President Franklin Roosevelt's commitment to enter the war, their attitude changed after the Nazis invaded Russia. At once, they supported the American war effort. The early antiwar opposition seemed counterintuitive for the Communists in Hamtramck. For many people in the city, the war began when Germany invaded Poland on September 1, 1939, and the Russians won no fans here when they followed the Nazis into

Workers of Hamtramck VOTE COMMUNIST---
Against Hunger and Fascism

For Mayor—
GEORGE KRISTALSKY

For Councilmen—
RICHARD RUFFINI   JENNIE ROMANIUK
CASS BAILEY   FRANK DZIUBIK
GEORGE MOSZCZYNSKI

For Treasurer—   For City Clerk—
EMIL SOBOL   MICHAEL ZACKLER

ROBOTNICY HAMTRAMCK Głosujcie na Komunistów
Przeciwko Głodowi i Faszyzmowi

Na Mayora—
GEORGE KRISTALSKY

Na Konsilmanów—
RICHARD RUFFINI   JENNIE ROMANIUK
CASS BAILEY   FRANK DZIUBIK
GEORGE MOSZCZYNSKI

Na Kasjera—   Na Klerka Miejskiego—
EMIL SOBOL   MICHAEL ZACKLER

(Over)

This page: The message was made in English and Polish. The Communists appealed to the workers who often were oppressed and suffered with nearly intolerable working and living conditions.

Poland sixteen days later, taking over half the country. The Russians further alienated local Poles after the war by setting up a puppet regime, once again denying Poland its independence.

The fear of the Red Menace was settling in like it had never before. Even prior to the war there had been action against the Communists. In February 1940, the Hamtramck police were called to the International Worker's Home on Yemans five times in fifty-two minutes in response to hecklers disrupting a meeting of the Communists. Kristalsky complained about "the disgraceful violation of our civil rights" to the common council. The council listened to Kristalsky's complaint and asked for a report from the police department, but it was clear that the issue wasn't going any further. John Matkowski, who was a member of the Hamtramck School Board and a heckler at the hall, also addressed the council, asking the city to tear down the Yemans hall. "We will not permit your kind to hold any meetings in Hamtramck," he said.

In August 1940, Councilman Frank Leach sponsored a resolution calling for the federal government to deny Communists the right to broadcast over the radio. "It allows Fifth Columnists and others preaching the doctrine of foreign totalitarian states to spread their seditious propaganda over the air under the guise of free speech," he said.

Periodically, after the war, the Communists would crop up in the press in one way or another. In a bizarre twist, charges of Communist infiltration of the Hamtramck Public School System were raised in June of 1947. The charges stemmed from an injunction filed against the school board, preventing it from making any appointments. The board believed child accounting director Anthony L. Kar was behind the order, although John Radwanski was listed as the plaintiff. Kar was under consideration to be appointed new superintendent. School trustee Vincent Sadlowski labeled Kar as a Communist and accused the Communists of trying to exercise power over the school board to insert their candidate (Kar) into the position. Whether this was political posturing or simple paranoia isn't clear, but the board did call for an anti-Communist rally to be held at Hamtramck High School. The school auditorium had seating for 600 but only about 300 people showed up. They were treated to a diatribe against Communism by Frank B. Sosnowski, a perennial Republican candidate for Congress. Kar was branded as a Communist with several speakers suggesting that he be sent to Russia. As school trustee Edward Koepk said, "He says he has the qualifications. Well, let him take those qualifications to Russia." He didn't, but neither did he become school superintendent.

That wasn't the school board's only contact with Communism. In May of 1949, the board went on record to ban Communists altogether because Communism "is directed towards world domination and control, with an especial avowed ambition to overthrow the government of the United States."

As the cold war deepened, anti-Communist sentiments grew, taking an alarming turn.

"There are known Communists in the city yards and local organizations," said Stanley Wolski, of the Hamtramck Allied Veterans Council, as he asked the common council to reactivate the police subversive activities squad in March of 1948. Police chief John Wojciszak said the department had two men checking on radical activities in the city. He wasn't kidding: in July of 1949, Anton Koshewoy was arrested on charges of having subversive associations. The arrest was made at the request of U.S. immigration authorities, who said Koshewoy, who had been born in Russia, came to America in 1922 and was a former president of the Workman's Co-Op restaurant on Yemans, a well-known Communist operation. He wasn't the only person arrested. In August 1949, John Sokol and Henry Podolski were arrested and held for deportation. Sokol was the manager of the Workman's Co-Op, and Podolski was a translator for Unity Press in Detroit. Both men were charged with being "members of organizations advocating the overthrow of the government by force or violence."

The case of John Zydok drew national attention as it dragged through the courts. Zydok was the head waiter at the Workman's Co-Op and also happened to be the financial secretary of the Russian sector of the Communist Party in Hamtramck. He was picked up in a national sweep of eighty-six of the nation's leading Communists. First released on $1,000 bond pending deportation hearings, the bond was revoked under the then new Internal Security Act that allowed the Justice Department to hold a person in custody if deemed a threat to national security.

Zydok was a genuine Communist operating in the community. He was one of many, in fact. In June 1949, police were besieged with calls from residents complaining that men were distributing fliers signed "The Communist Front of Hamtramck," deriding capitalists who "have cheated our people long enough." Those fliers, however, were placed on house porches anonymously, and when the men distributing them were approached they fled to waiting cars and sped away.

Incidents like that stoked anti-Communist sentiments. They made the enemy not only real, but in the neighborhood. Interestingly, the anonymous approach showed how the situation had deteriorated for the Communists in the space of the decade. In 1940, the Hamtramck Communists conducted an open house-to-house signature-collecting campaign to have the party placed on the 1940 ballot. A decade later they were secretly distributing literature.

Response to the Communists was intensifying. In July 1950, the city employees' union asked the council to require that all city workers sign affidavits swearing they were not Communists, and that those who refused to sign "be dealt with accordingly." The union also urged the council to prohibit the sale or distribution to the general public all "subversive or Communistic literature." The council passed the oath, extending it to all members of the city's library, housing, zoning and recreation commissions and all part-time and seasonal recreation employees.

The net was widening. Even well-established figures came under attack. Congressman George Sadowski, who represented Hamtramck, was charged with allowing a Communist to use his congressional free mailing privileges. Sadowski admitted he sent George Wuchinich, of Pittsburgh, 2,000 copies of a speech he made calling for the lifting of trade restrictions with Iron Curtain countries. He also sent along 2,000 postage-free envelopes.

"His views agreed exactly with mine," Sadowski said of Wuchinich. "I like what he had to say about foreign trade. I didn't care whether his political views were different from anyone else."

Wuchinich had been identified as a Communist by an FBI informer speaking before the House Un-American Activities Committee.

In the early 1950s, the Red Scare hysteria seemed to have peaked, at least locally. Perhaps the threat lessened with the ending of the Korean War, which had been used by some to stir anti-Communist fervor. Certainly the discrediting of Communist-baiter senator Joseph McCarthy in 1954 had an impact. The raids on the Communists' hall on Yemans and the Workman's Co-Op restaurant must have thinned the ranks of the Communists. Or perhaps the hard-working folks of Hamtramck realized the Communists actually played little to no role in their daily lives and really weren't a threat. Calling for workers to sign loyalty oaths did nothing to improve the quality of life for those workers or the community as a whole. The Communists didn't evaporate and residents didn't entirely cease to care, but their priorities shifted. A stunning example of that was shown in the election of 1954. For weeks prior to the election, congressional candidate and former mayor Rudolph Tenerowicz ran a series of dramatic full-page ads in the *Citizen* newspaper with such titles as, "The Amazing story of the 800,000,000

Slaves, or: The Soviet Slave Empire," and "Communism in Action." They were designed to show how the Republican Party bravely had stood up to the Communist threat, while the Democratic Party had been infiltrated by Communists. "We must stop bolstering imperialism and Communism," Tenerowicz proclaimed in his newspaper ads. Tenerowicz himself was a former Democrat who had served in Congress from 1939 to 1943; he lost a bid to return to Congress in 1946. He said he lost because the Communist Party "ordered" his defeat. In actuality, it was because he had lost support of the labor unions, changed parties and became a Republican, which was political suicide in the overwhelmingly Democratic Hamtramck.

His attitude hadn't changed in his return bid for Congress in November 1954, but the results for the once-incredibly popular politician were stunning. He was defeated by incumbent Democrat Thaddeus Machrowicz 12,574 to 1,264 votes.

Tenerowicz's anti-Communist diatribes carried no weight.

More and more Hamtramckans in the 1950s would be concerned with issues of parking, polio and the myriad problems of an aging community. The Red Scare seemed to be paling, but the Communists never really went away. For many years their newspapers could be found in a sales rack at the corner of Jos. Campau and Holbrook, and you can still find copies of the *Workers World* newspaper around town. From time to time, news items about the Communists would appear in the other local newspapers. As late as the 1970s, radicals operated a secret office on the second floor of a Jos. Campau building.

In 1981, the Communists made their presence known, appropriately on May 1, or May Day. It wasn't an impressive showing, however; just some highly visible graffiti painted on the side of the Holbrook–Jos. Campau building. It read: "We're proletariats—not Americans. Our flag is red—not red, white and blue."

But the words didn't last long, and there was no sign of who wrote them. So where did all the Communists go?

Some are still around. In fact, they are active in Hamtramck today, although they keep a relatively low profile. But there is something telling in the ultimate fate of George Kristalsky. The perennial Communist Party candidate for political offices in Hamtramck bought a two-family house on Grandy Street, just outside of Hamtramck, and embraced the capitalist lifestyle.

By 1949, he owned a drugstore on McNichols Avenue in nearby Detroit.

CHAPTER 5

Forever Bad

The young mom sat of her front porch on a warm summer evening. She cradled her daughter, rocking gently, the clacking of the passing streetcars providing a backdrop to the serene setting. It is a memory that child would remember nearly ninety years later, long after the streetcars—and mom—were gone.

In those days, the 1920s, Hamtramck was a landscape of sharp contrasts. Most of the houses were the same, and the population was fairly uniform. Most folks were hard working and law abiding, but those that were bad were really bad.

Through the decades, Hamtramck produced an impressive rogues' gallery that often shocked the community—and even the nation—as they spread their mayhem far beyond the city's borders.

Here's a sampling:

WHO KILLED HERMANN SCHMIDT?

When the immigrant influx began in 1910, it quickly turned Hamtramck from a dusty, mainly farming town into a major industrial city within the space of ten years. Rows of houses were thrown up at a furious rate as neighborhoods rose to house the growing population. The Village of Hamtramck was completely unprepared to handle the wrenching changes the community was experiencing. It was a traumatic period; and the events of February 17, 1917, must have been shocking to a town that just a few years earlier was little more than farmland and where the only gunshots heard may have come from an occasional hunter.

It started innocently. A group of people started throwing snowballs at two men near the village police station on Jos. Campau Avenue near Grayling Street. Words were exchanged, and one of the men swung at a youth. He missed and fell to the ground. As he rose, he drew a gun and began firing. Three youths, age eleven, thirteen, fourteen, and a man, age twenty, were struck.

It's not clear how serious they were hurt, but the old records carry at least one notation of "not expected to live."

Police officer Hermann Schmidt was in the police station when he heard the shots. He ran outside and began chasing one of the men. The other man ran in another direction and was never heard of again.

Schmidt continued his chase when the gunman ducked behind a utility pole, turned and fired, hitting Schmidt in the chest, killing him.

No one was able to identify the man or his companion. The case drifted into history but briefly resurfaced in August 1943, when a tip led police to reopen the case. Incredibly, the police were able to locate some of the people involved in the original shooting, including a man identified as the shooter. He was questioned but denied everything, including even hearing of the shooting. The police placed the man in a lineup, but the witnesses were unable to identify him. He was released and drifted into history.

The case remains unsolved.

BETTER OFF DEAD

John Deering was thirty-nine when he was arrested in Hamtramck in 1938 on suspicion of robbery. He had already spent seventeen years in prison and vowed that his next stay there would be a short one.

No, he wouldn't escape—although he had already done that once before in a blaze of gunfire. He was going to take another way out. In jail, he confessed to the murder of Oliver R. Meredith Jr. during a robbery in Salt Lake City, Utah. He was extradited to Utah where he stood trial for first-degree murder. During the trial he maintained that he was a hopeless criminal and would be "better off dead." The court agreed. He was convicted of murder and given the option of being hanged or shot by firing squad.

"I prefer to be shot," Deering said. He had a reason for his choice.

"When I was a kid raising hell everyone told me I'd end up on the gallows, so I thought I'd fool them. Also, there's an old saying like 'live by the sword and die by the sword.'"

In early November 1938, Deering was taken to the prison courtyard, strapped in a chair and a bag was placed over his head. A target was placed over his heart and five deputies pointed their rifles at it.

On the orders of Sheriff S. Grant Young, they fired. Although it was bullets that killed him, he died by the sword.

A JUDICIAL HANG-UP

It's unlikely that Anthony Chebatoris had any idea of the dilemma he put Governor Frank Murphy in when he set himself up for the death penalty. Nor is it likely the "sneering, hard-bitten little Pole" from Hamtramck, as he was described in the national press, cared.

Chebatoris was thirty-seven in 1938 when he faced the death penalty after killing a truck driver while fleeing from a bank in Midland, Michigan, which he had just robbed with an accomplice, fellow Hamtramckan Jack Gracey. Chebatoris and his pal had shot two guards in the Chemical State Saving Bank, but it was the killing of the truck driver passing by that drew the death penalty.

Gracey had his brains blown out by a local dentist, Dr. Frank L. Hardy, who witnessed the robbery and fired his hunting rifle from his office above the bank as the pair fled. Chebatoris was wounded by Hardy but recovered.

Michigan had abolished the death penalty a century earlier; however, bank robbery was—and still is—a federal crime punishable under federal guidelines. And committing murder in the process of robbing a bank carries the ultimate penalty.

Chebatoris was scheduled to hang at the Federal Detention Farm in Milan, Michigan, in July 1938. But that didn't sit well with Governor Frank Murphy, who wanted to preserve Michigan's tradition of not executing criminals in its boundaries. He appealed directly to President Franklin Roosevelt to have the execution moved to another state. Roosevelt turned the matter over to the Department of Justice to see if anything could be done. In fact, no state that prohibits capital punishment can be forced to carry one out—but there was a hitch. Michigan's constitution specified that the death penalty was prohibited in all cases, except "high treason."

That meant the hangman's noose was not totally banned. Federal judge Arthur J. Tuttle, who presided over Chebatoris's trial, was asked to intervene, but he said, "I have neither the power nor the inclination….I think it would be unfair to suggest that people of neighboring States are less humane than are the people of our own."

In July 1938, executioner Phil Hanna, described as a "gentleman farmer" from Epworth, Illinois, made the somber trip to Milan, and Chebatoris's life of crime came to an abrupt end.

Governor Murphy was not happy. "Michigan has led the world in the civilized attitude toward criminals. The hanging today was a blot on our century-old tradition, but I hope that it will have the effect of helping to abolish capital punishment from all the states in the Union," he said.

THE MOST GORY DEATH

For decades Kanas Hall stood stoically at the corner of Conant and Evaline Streets until it was torn apart by a tornado in 1997. During its long life, it had hosted thousands of political rallies, dances and parties of all sorts. It was also the site of what was described as one of the bloodiest killings in Hamtramck's history.

The story unraveled in January 1937, when Mitchell Karaskiewicz, age twenty, broke down under police interrogation and admitted he had killed Paul Kolak, a night watchman at the hall.

Karaskiewicz, who lived at 11668 Moran, a handful of blocks north of the hall, already had a troubled past. He had served eighteen months of a one- to-five year sentence for car theft. He was paroled from the Detroit House of Corrections and had numerous other run-ins with the law on a variety of petty charges.

But early on a Sunday, he entered the world of big-time crime: homicide.

He told police this story: Earlier that evening, he had been at a party in Warren and came to Kanas Hall at about 1:30 a.m. Sunday, January 24, because there was a dance going on. In those days, dances were common affairs and almost every hall hosted them, especially on a Saturday night. Karaskiewicz's sister, Virginia, was among those attending the dance, but he stayed until almost everyone else had left. Finally, only he and Kolak were left in the hall. Karaskiewicz relates what happened next in his own words:

> *I talked 20 minutes with Kolak at the bar in the basement. I then went to his room (Kolak lived in the hall) and fell asleep. Later Kolak woke me up and asked me what I was doing. I told him I was the one who helped him at the*

Dances were a popular form of entertainment throughout Hamtramck, especially during the 1920s and 1930s. Kanas Hall was a typical venue, which would feature acts like Howard's Detroit Collegians.

hall. He told me I better get out, and he spilled a glass of beer on me. I grabbed for the glass in his hand and started to run upstairs. He chased me and finally caught me beside the stage. We fought a while and I must have pushed him because he fell to the bottom of the stairs and hit his head. I was scared and ran to the check room next to the ticket office and hid there for 10 or 15 minutes.

I finally came out and found him lying in blood. I saw him get up and pick up a coat. He used it to wipe his face of blood. I asked him, "Are you hurt?" and he came up after me. I ran to the other side of the stage. He got ahold of me there but I jerked away and ran to the front. He came after me. I tore away and pushed him into a pipe and he fell. Then as I tried to run back into the hall, he grabbed for my legs, got ahold of one and held on so tight one of my shoes came off. I took the shoe away and left through the side door.

It must have been late because people were going to church. I went to a candy store on Conant and bought two bottles of pop. I drank them and went home.

Kanas Hall was the site of many dances—and one homicide. The hall stood closed for years before it was destroyed by Hamtramck's only tornado in July 1997.

Kolak's body was discovered at 10:00 a.m. by another watchman who worked with Kolak. He called Joseph Maj, owner of the hall, who called police.

They found a grisly scene, a trail of blood leading to Kolak's body, his head split open and blood soaked.

Police tied Karaskiewicz to the crime through his coat. They found it on the stage and in the pocket was a coat-check tag with his address on it.

They went to his house and found him in bed, stained with Kolak's blood.

For two days after his arrest, Karaskiewicz told the police nothing. But on his way to the prosecutor's office he broke down and spilled the story. It was a good thing he did; in light of the gory details, instead of getting hit with a first-degree murder charge, Karaskiewicz was charged with manslaughter.

And he even managed to beat that rap. A jury of four men and two women at a Wayne County coroner's inquest deliberated for twenty-five minutes before coming back with a verdict that Kolak "died as the result of an accident."

The police weren't able to shake Karaskiewicz's story and prove that he deliberately killed Kolak.

Minutes after the verdict, Karaskiewicz stepped out of the courtroom—and into history—as a free man.

THE MOST SHOCKING MURDER

Hamtramck can be a hard town, but the rape and murder of seventeen-year-old Bernice Onisko stunned even the most hardened Hamtramckans in what was likely to most notorious murder in the history of the city.

The story came to light early on a Sunday morning in March 1937 when the body of Onisko was found by Bernice Kowalczyk behind her house at 2615 Botsford Street. Onisko had been raped and strangled with her own scarf, which was found stuffed in her mouth, apparently to muffle her screams.

Onisko was a pretty, slender girl with blue eyes and short bobbed hair, fashionable for the time but hardly enticing. She weighed less than 100 pounds and would not have been able to put up much resistance to a determined attacker. Her mother described her as a "quiet, shy girl who didn't have a boyfriend and was a devout Christian." In fact, she was on her way home from church when she was attacked and killed.

The murder of Bernice Onisko shocked the community perhaps more than any other crime has, even to this day.

"She was a home girl and a church girl," said her mother, Cecilia Onisko. "She never had a boy friend and she never went out at night."

Bernice had graduated from St. Ladislaus High School the previous June and had been an honor student, even wining a medal for her typing skills. Her father had died the previous July after a long illness, and she worked to help support the family, which was in a tenuous condition—already suffering like so many others in the Great Depression. Compounding the family woes, Bernice had been hit in the face with a baseball as a child and suffered from persistent pain. She had undergone an operation to alleviate the pain and was planning a second surgery.

With the help of her mother, friends and people who had seen her just prior to her death, police were quickly able to construct a timetable of events.

"Saturday she did the housework. She got dinner and after we ate she said her prayers," her mother said. "She was making a mission to ask God to give me back my health. Before she went to church she prayed for me. She prayed her own operation would be successful." Bernice left her house at about 7:15 p.m. for the eight-block walk to St. Ladislaus Church. She was accompanied by her younger sister, Loretta, age eleven.

Father A.A. Majewski later told police he saw Bernice sitting alone in the church, and a neighbor said he saw Bernice leave the church at the end of the services at 8:55 p.m. What happened next could be surmised. As Bernice neared the alley between Botsford and Commor Streets, she was approached from behind by a man who grabbed her and pulled her into the alley. He forced her scarf into her mouth and dragged her in between two sheds where he partially ripped her clothes off and assaulted her, finally strangling her. It was a brief, violent encounter—but quiet. No one reported hearing anything. And like the mist, the killer vanished into the darkness of that cold, dismal alley.

The frenzy began the next morning when Bernice's body was found. Word spread quickly about her gruesome death. People gathered at the crime scene; everyone was talking about the murder. Rumors swirled: someone said a priest was responsible. Onisko's cousin, who lived in the upper flat of the Onisko home, was given a lie detector test but was not held by police.

Adding to the frenzy were some bizarre twists. Three days after the murder, Cecilia Onisko received a handwritten note from someone confessing to the murder. "Yes I did it but only after she bit my face and two fingers. She was like a tiger," it read. "When you get this I will be out of the state. What can I say more, what can I say….just amen."

A fingerprint was found on the paper,but no match could be found.

This page: Mrs. Bernice Kowalczyk points out the spot in the alley behind Botsford Street where Bernice's body was found in March 1937. Decades later, Hamtramckan Rebecca Binno Savage points to the same spot. The murder remains unsolved.

On Friday, March 12, 1937, Hamtramck witnessed one of the largest funerals in its history. Huge crowds turned out at the Onisko house and at St. Ladislaus Church for the ceremony. A large procession bore her body to Mount Olivet Cemetery for burial.

Even the Hamtramck Common Council took note. Councilman Fred Dibble proposed that the city offer a $1,000 reward for the capture of the killer. That, however, was a little too steep for the council as a whole, and Dibble's motion was not supported. But when Councilman Walter Kanar knocked the reward down to $500, the measure passed unanimously.

"This isn't a question of how much it's worth to get the killer, but $500 is a whole lot more within our means," city attorney William Cohen said. Council president George Banish said offering a reward would speed up the capture of the killer.

It didn't.

In fact, the investigation dragged on with no meaningful results. Within days of the killing, more than twenty men were hauled in by police as suspects.

Stanley Lachowicz, twenty-four, was typical. He was arrested on a tip from a shoeshine boy who said he shined his shoes at his stand at Jos. Campau and Carpenter at 10 p.m. the night of the murder. Muddy shoes were enough to implicate him. But after a day of questioning, he was released by police.

Pressure quickly mounted on police to break the case. Within another week, a squadron of Hamtramck detectives and uniformed officers brought in another thirty suspects for questioning. Among them was Peter Pancheson, described as a "slightly demented" Sandusky, Ohio, man. Police in surrounding areas outside Hamtramck joined in the investigation, all with no results. Detroit handwriting expert Earl Stevens was brought in to look over the voter registration forms of every Hamtramck man younger than twenty-seven to compare the signature to the handwritten "confession" note Onisko's mother had received. No match was found. The investigation was going nowhere. Then in late April police seemed to get a break. Twenty-one-year-old Edward Belecki, of Brinkert Street in north Detroit, confessed. But the story quickly fell apart. Police examined clothing at his home and found no signs of blood or mud. Further, it was determined that Belecki was in another town the night of the killing.

Belecki had given police a detailed account of the killing, but later admitted he had made it up from what he had heard in radio reports of the crime. The incident was an embarrassment for the police, who had made much of the confession, announcing they had cracked the case.

And that was it. The case went completely cold: no more tips; no arrests; no leads.

There were further stirrings of activity. In January 1938, Detroit waitress Emma Mahn was murdered in a manner that immediately made police suspicious that the Onisko killer was responsible.

"Miss Mahn's killing is similar to the murder of the Onisko girl in that the slayer made an attempt to strangle the victim with a piece of her clothing," said police inspector Paul Wencel, chief of the homicide squad.

"A scarf was stuffed down the Onisko girl's throat, and her belt tied around her neck. Miss Mahn died from blows to the head, but her belt had been wrapped around her throat, apparently before the slayer discovered she was dead. The Onisko girl's body was found near a beer garden and Miss Mahn had just a left a beer garden with Norton."

Norton was Clarence Norton, a thirty-year-old Detroit man who confessed to killing Mahn.

"In each case the victim's shoes figured prominently. One of Emma Mahn's shoes was found near her body, and we knew Norton fractured her skull with the heel. Miss Onisko's shoe lay near her body, as if her killer had intended to use it as a weapon, but found the scarf sufficient," Wencel said. "At any rate, the coincidence is too striking to ignore."

But it was not strong enough to prove a connection. Norton denied any involvement in the Onisko murder. After questioning Norton, Hamtramck detective Barney Nowicki concluded he was telling the truth.

It was another dead end.

On Sunday, March 6, 1938—almost one year after Bernice Onisko's body was found—there still was no trace of the killer. But no one had forgotten the crime, least of all her grief-stricken mother. A memorial Mass was held for Bernice Onisko at St. Ladislaus Church. The wounds were still fresh for Bernice's mother.

"She can't keep back the tears of a broken heart that never healed," the *New Deal* newspaper reported. "Every thought or recollection of the crime opens a fresh wound. She prays reverently that the maniac who killed her beloved daughter be brought to justice."

Sadly, he never was.

COUNT GYPPER

He spoke six languages and possessed a "magnetic personality." With a past that read like it was written in a Russian novel, "Count" Mikolaj Sokolowski was one of the most interesting criminals ever to grace the Hamtramck jail.

At the time of his arrest in March 1936, he was fifty-two years old and had already led a life that would rival any character from fiction. He really wasn't a count, but he was an engineer in the Russian army after the revolution of 1917. When the Bolsheviks came to power and the Soviet Union was created, he was forced to flee. He settled in China where he became acquainted with some exporters. From them he gained enough experience to pass himself off as a dealer in rare rugs, church artifacts and—of all things—sausage casings from China.

But his real skill was in exporting money from his victims' wallets. Between 1925 and 1927, he was suspected of swindling some $30,000 from area residents and merchants, convincing them to invest in his business. Promising a huge return on their investment, the count simply pocketed their money. When the police began to take an interest in his affairs, he left the country and settled in Poland, although authorities in China, the Soviet Union, Argentina and Poland were on his trail. In 1935, he returned to the Detroit area where he ingratiated himself with the Polish community by giving speeches on the cause of Poland.

He also operated a clever Ponzi scheme called engagement circles. This involved engaged couples who agreed to pay him $10, for which they would receive $250 when they actually got married. The only stipulation was that they had to find another couple to replace them in the circle. Things began to fall apart when one couple tried to collect the $250, and the count was unable to pay them. When the groom said he was going to the police, the count gave him $75.

The count dropped out of sight, but finally he was tracked to a house just outside Hamtramck where his wife was staying. He was booked by police, but immigration authorities stepped in. He was charged with being an illegal alien and was set to be deported to Europe when he requested to be sent to China. His request was not honored.

Entirely unremorseful, the count told his victims, "You willingly gave me the money, so why should you kick?"

BORN BAD

When Roman Usiondek put a gun to his head and blew his brains out in a parking lot, he brought to an end one of the most impressive criminal careers in the history of Hamtramck. Usiondek was beyond bad. Probably psychopathic, he had no regard for the law or human life. If you stood in his way, you died. In fact, he would go out of his way to kill.

Usiondek first made his name in the world of big-time crime with the murder of Peter Kubert on May 23, 1942, while Usiondek was a member of a particularly fierce holdup gang that specialized in robbing bars.

The bold robbers, who were probably already responsible for a series of earlier robberies—including the Lumpkin–Wyandotte Bar, the Columbia Café on Jacob Street and Bill's Bar on Conant Avenue—went on a particularly violent robbery spree on the night of Friday, May 22. That night and going into the early morning they hit three bars. At 9:45 p.m., they robbed a bar on St. Aubin Street, taking $100 from the proprietor. Police got a call about the robbery on their newly installed car radios and

Now known as Shananigan's, this was Peter Kubert's popular bar back in the 1940s. Located on Carpenter Avenue, it is on the border with Detroit and was a tempting target for Roman Usiondek and his gang.

quickly located the robbers speeding north on St. Aubin but lost them in heavy traffic.

Three hours later, the robbers struck again. They hit Sonny's Cafe at 12424 Van Dyke in Detroit. They took $1,600, including $700 in checks from proprietor Louis "Sonny" Popp.

At 1:20 a.m., they were back in Hamtramck, entering Peter Kubert's Bar, at 3216 Carpenter Avenue, at Hamtramck's northern border with Detroit. Billed as "Hamtramck's No. 1 Fun Spot," Peter Kubert's Bar was an especially popular night spot. It was where you could hear the music of Clyde Grant on the piano and listen to Mary Lane, the singing waitress, and "Smiling" Al Feda, the singing bartender. Everyone joined in the entertainment on Friday nights at a community singalong.

The music stopped when the four men wearing handkerchiefs over their faces and brandishing blue steel handguns burst into Kubert's bar. They quickly herded the seventeen patrons on site into a back room and rifled the cash register. But it held only $400. That wasn't enough, and they demanded more from Kubert. That's when Kubert made a big mistake: he sarcastically pointed to a pile of nickels and dimes on the bar. The thieves were not amused, and one fired his gun, striking Kubert in the stomach. Kubert leaped behind the bar and grabbed his own gun. He came up blazing, firing five shots but, dazed by his wound, his shots went wild; later it was learned that he had struck one of the robbers. They responded with their own bullets, hitting Kubert in the abdomen and right arm. Kubert went down, and the thieves ran out. The police arrived quickly on the scene. Kubert was taken to nearby St. Francis Hospital where he was treated, given several blood infusions and listed in fair condition.

Kubert never lost consciousness and told his wife, Sophia, that the thieves had threatened "to shoot his guts out" unless he produced more money. Kubert's condition deteriorated as he developed peritonitis and he died a week after being shot.

The crime shocked and outraged the city. Kubert wasn't just a popular businessman with a friendly place. He was a civic-minded citizen who contributed to the town. Ironically, on the evening he was shot, his picture and a story appeared in the *Citizen* newspaper noting how he and his wife, Sophie, had hosted a party for Manistee judge John D. Kruse and John Zaigor, president of the Class C Club in Manistee, at the bar the previous Friday. Judge Kruse even gave Kubert a large key to the city made of salt. (Manistee was once known for its salt production.)

Peter Kubert (center) was a well-known person in Hamtramck. He often participated in civic events. Here he is pictured with Judge John Kruse (left) of Manistee and John Zaigor, Manistee Class C Club president. The photo was taken a week before Kubert's murder.

The common council offered a $500 reward for the arrest of the killers. "As long as these killers roam the streets, no one in Hamtramck is safe," said common council president Walter Serement, who proposed the award. He had sought a $100 reward, but Councilman Frank Sosnowski upped it to $500, and the council approved it unanimously.

"If that amount isn't enough, I'm sure the businessmen of this community will spontaneously join in making the reward larger by contributing to the fund," Serement said. "Mr. Kubert was a fine citizen, an asset to this city, and certainly not deserving of the fate which was meted out by merciless bandits."

Two squads of investigators from Hamtramck and one from Detroit were assigned to the case. They got a break when a witness said he saw one of the robbers without his face covered and noted he had a large mole. It wasn't much, but it was enough for the streetwise cops who knew every neighborhood thug. They quickly brought in Rudolph Madaj, thirty-five, in for questioning. A tip led the police to Emil Jaworski, twenty-six, who didn't have a criminal record but was known to the local underworld. By

September, four men were charged with Kubert's death: Madaj, Jaworski, James Lynch, thirty-four, and Roman Usiondek. A fifth man, Henry Hill, admitted to taking part in the robbery, but he became a state witness.

They went to trial in January 1943 charged with robbery and murder before Wayne County Circuit Court judge Theodore J. Richter. A jury of eight men and five women listened to a week of testimony before beginning deliberations, but it didn't take them long to hand down guilty verdicts to Usiondek, Madaj and Lynch. Jaworski was acquitted, having produced an alibi that he was elsewhere when the crime was committed.

The three were sentenced to life in prison.

Roman Usiondek's life of crime did not end with the murder of Peter Kubert. Born in 1916, as a juvenile he had been sentenced to fifteen months in the Boys' Industrial School for breaking and entering.

In 1936, he was sentenced to five to twenty years in Jackson prison for breaking and entering. He was paroled four years later but was back in jail in six months for violating his parole. Six months after that, he was back on the street. It was also believed but not proved that he had shot underworld figure Frankie Reid in the face after boldly walking up to him while he was standing on Woodward Avenue and asking for a cigarette and match.

Eleven years after being sent to prison for the murder of Kubert, Usiondek escaped from the prison at Jackson, setting off a massive manhunt. So fierce was Usiondek's reputation that families of the people involved in his 1942 trial were placed under guard. They had a lot to fear: when Usiondek had been sentenced to life in prison for killing Kubert, he glared at assistant prosecutor A. Tom Pasieczny and said, "I'll be back and you'll be number one on my list."

Hamtramck police captain Walter Jaros said, "Usiondek is a cold blooded murderer who swore vengeance against all of the witnesses who testified against him at his trial. Unless he had softened during his years in prison, and his escape proves he has not, I fear he will attempt to carry out his threat."

He was on his way back and to make things worse, he had somehow gotten a gun.

Usiondek was one of thirteen inmates to escape from the prison through a storm sewer. He and four other escapees soon broke into the home of Joseph Watts in Jackson, not far from the prison, forcing his wife, Mary Lou, to make coffee and cook food while they bathed and shaved.

Also in the house was Mrs. Watts's friend, Helen Gilbert, who was waiting for Don Peck to pick her up for a date, and fourteen-year-old babysitter, Mary Bobber. When Peck arrived, he found himself drawn into the drama.

At first the escapees were going to take Mary Bobber as hostage, but the adults pleaded with them, and instead they took Mrs. Watts and Gilbert. Before they left, however, they made a critical error in asking Mr. Watts the way to Indiana.

Later, Mrs. Watts and Gilbert told a harrowing tale of eluding the police to Ed Smith of the *Jackson-Citizen Patriot* newspaper:

> *"We headed south on M-60 at 70 or 60 miles an hour," Mrs. Watts told Smith. "We ran into the first roadblock about 15 miles from home, but they saw it in time and backtracked to the first side road.*
>
> *"We were in constant fear—not of the convicts—but we were afraid a state police car might come alongside and open fire. Then too, we thought we might get into trouble for helping them escape because we were sort of giving them directions when they asked us.*
>
> *"From then it was one set of back roads after another. We finally ran out gas at Climax (about 15 miles west of Battle Creek). There was a filling station open and we pulled in.*
>
> *"You'll be okay if you don't make a sound, they told us, and we kept quiet.*
>
> *"A state police car passed us as we drove from the gas station, but they didn't notice us. Then it was more back roads until we drove almost to Flint and then Detroit—always on back roads."*
>
> As dire as the situation was, Mrs. Watts noted that the convicts actually seemed to be friendly—with the exception of Usiondek.
>
> *"It was funny," she said. "All of them except the one called Usiondek were almost kind. One time I sort of bowed my head trying to stay awake and once of the convicts asked if I was sick.*
>
> *"Once they talked about the break and one of them said he felt like turning himself in after they were outside. He said there were too many to be successful.*
>
> *"Whenever they wanted to talk about their plans, though, they stopped the car and talked outside. Once they skidded into a ditch because there was ice on the road. Then Usiondek went wild, screaming about Dowling's driving and waving a gun. It seemed as if they were afraid of him."*

They arrived in Detroit about 6:30 a.m. Usiondek and another escapee got out of the car at Seven Mile Road and Southfield Road. The other two drove a little farther down the road, then gave Mrs. Watts and Gilbert two dollars and told them not to contact the police for at least fifteen minutes and disappeared into the early morning darkness. Gilbert and Watts drove to a gas station near Wyoming and Joy Roads where they called police.

Police immediately mounted a massive manhunt. Six teams of detectives were assigned to track down Usiondek and his pals. It didn't take long to get results. Eight of the thirteen escapees were back in jail before daybreak. One had been caught hiding in the coal bin of a hotel near the prison. Six others were captured when they tried to run a roadblock and smashed their car.

Two days later, on December 23, Usiondek and Dowling were captured in a hotel room in Richmond, Indiana. Two cruising police officers became suspicious when they spotted a car with Michigan plates and containing two half-eaten loaves of bread.

Usiondek's life of crime was still far from over. In 1965, he was released from prison after appealing on a technicality his conviction of the Kubert killing. He had been re-sentenced, credited with time served and released. In 1967, he was back to practicing his particular brand of mayhem.

He had a new partner, Edward Emrick, another Hamtramckan who almost matched Usiondek for sheer meanness. Emrick had a police record that stretched back to the 1920s but reached its peak in 1952 when he killed Detroit police detective Russell Blanchard. He spent thirteen years in prison but was granted a new trial, found guilty of manslaughter and soon released from prison.

Emrick was one of the men who had escaped with Usiondek from prison in 1953. Two of a kind, they began working together with another accomplice, George Patro, who also had a long record of major crimes, including kidnapping and robbery. On a warm July night in 1967, they burglarized the JoAnn Supper Club on Eight Mile Road, about two miles north of Hamtramck.

Things, however, would not go as Emrick and Usiondek planned. Early that morning, a silent alarm went off at the supper club, alerting the Detroit police and the alarm company. Soon a police officer and company employee arrived at the club. A watchman, speaking through the closed the door said "nothing was wrong." But the officer heard suspicious movements inside and broke a window. The watchman said he was being held hostage, and three shots were fired. The officer called for backup, drawing nine scout cars to the scene. At that point Emrick attempted to escape, running across Eight Mile Road. He made it to a parking lot when he collapsed and died, brought down by a policeman's bullet.

Usiondek fared only a little better. He had been holding the watchman as a shield when the police broke into the building. An officer shot Usiondek once, hitting him in the stomach.

The JoAnn Supper Club on Eight Mile Road in Detroit is now closed. It was just one of Usiondek's crime scenes.

The night watchman told police he had been tricked into opening the door when someone yelled that the roof was on fire. When he opened the door, Usiondek, Emrick and Patro rushed in. But they didn't realize that in doing so, they tripped the silent alarm.

However, it would take more than a gut shot to stop Usiondek.

In 1974, he was paroled, quickly sent back to prison for a parole violation and was back out in 1978. Early in the morning of December 17, 1979, Usiondek met Charles Omela at the door of Club 77 on Jos. Campau and forced him inside at gunpoint. The two joined bar employee Henry Kot, forty-two, and after robbing Omela and Kot, Usiondek forced them into a back room where he shot Kot once in the head, killing him. He also shot at Omela but the bullet was deflected by a beer case that Omela grabbed and threw up to cover his head. Usiondek fled, disappearing into the streets.

Police released a composite drawing and immediately received a flood of calls from former police officers who had worked on the Kubert killing. Usiondek was now the prime suspect in the Kot killing, but where was he?

After he walked out of Club 77, he disappeared. Those who knew him couldn't or wouldn't say where he was. Police theorized he left the area. But he wouldn't stay away for long.

He made his final appearance eight months later.

Shortly after 6 p.m. on Saturday, July 26, 1980, Usiondek went to Roy's Market at 10308 Jos. Campau. Although owner Roy J. Ficaro was closing the market, he allowed Usiondek to enter. Whether they knew each other is not clear, nor is it known what they argued about. But both men were seen coming out of the store, and Ficaro pushed Usiondek. Usiondek pulled a gun, firing once and hitting Ficaro in the face. He died instantly.

Usiondek fled across Jos. Campau, down Trowbridge Street and through the alley toward Caniff Avenue. Suddenly he turned and fired at a woman driving into the alley from Trowbridge. The woman was struck in the chest and was later rushed to Henry Ford Hospital in serious condition.

Usiondek was in line for a different fate.

He ran into a parking lot next to St. Ladislaus convent across Caniff. There he was cornered by police, who had rapidly converged on the scene. An officer fired at Usiondek. He shot back. But there was nowhere else to run. All the years in prison, the killings, the robberies came to an end in that parking lot.

Usiondek put the gun to his head and pulled the trigger.

Ficaro had operated Roy's Market for sixteen years, and was well liked in the community. His death was shocking.

"It's a shame to lose this man," police chief John Sitek said. "It's really a sad loss when you lose people like this."

No such words were said for Roman Usiondek, Hamtramck's worst criminal.

Roman Usiondek's last moments were spent in this area, at the St. Ladislaus convent on Caniff Avenue, where he shot himself.

ROGUES' GALLERY

Some are so hard-bitten you can see the fierceness in their eyes. Others simply look like lost souls. The Roarin' Twenties were roarin' indeed in Hamtramck. The police had their hands full rounding up hardened criminals, petty thieves, prostitutes, drunks and brawlers. The police mug shot books from the era are filled with hundreds of photos.

Here's a sampling, all from the 1920s. We know their names, but their fates have long been lost to history. Yet, just looking into their eyes tells a story:

Mabelle Browden.

Stanley Drozdowski, aka "Hard Boiled."

Joseph Jagosz, aka "Sheephead" and "Whitey."

Shirley Hughes, aka "Shirley Lyons."

Rudolph Strausse, aka Rudolph "Lucky" Brown.

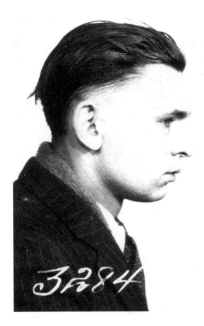

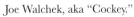

Joe Walchek, aka "Cockey."

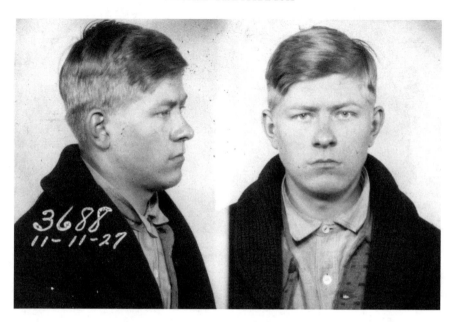

John Jascincki.

Dorothy Lynch.

CHAPTER 6

Redemption

O utrageous would not be too strong a word to use to describe the wild days of Hamtramck, as mayors were sent to prison; police officers were indicted for protecting graft; and school board members were charged with bribery for attempting to undermine what had been one of the finest school systems in the nation.

But this must be put into perspective. It's true that the school system was threatened by corrupt board members, but that shouldn't overshadow the fact that it was such a fine system.

In fact, while the city generated headlines for its exploits on the wrong side of the law, it was making tremendous contributions to the nation in the areas of education, entertainment, sports, science, labor and industry. These were routinely overlooked and ignored outside the city's perimeter. The frustration with that was evident early on and voiced all though the years. Periodically, city officials would be infuriated by some article or another that appeared in a major magazine. But while the national press paid occasional notice to Hamtramck, it was the continuing barrage by the Detroit media that stung the most. It wasn't just because the press seemed to revel in the woes of Hamtramck, but it also blatantly ignored what good was evident. A prime example was shown in 1938 when the city held a major celebration commemorating the 150th anniversary of the adoption of the U.S. Constitution. A huge parade with 2,500 participating traveled down Jos. Campau to Keyworth Stadium where 15,000 people attended a patriotic program.

With the election of Dr. Stephen Skrzycki (left) as mayor in 1942, Hamtramck turned its back on its wild past. Administering the oath of office to him is city clerk Albert J. Zak, who would succeed Skrzycki as mayor in 1952 and continue the tradition of clean government.

This rated scant mention in the daily newspapers, which in turn prompted outrage among city officials. In a long letter to the *Detroit News*, the members of the Hamtramck United States Sesquicentennial Committee, headed by Judge Nicholas Gronkowski and school superintendent M.A. Kopka, blasted the press.

The day following this patriotic celebration the Hamtramck residents furiously scanned the pages of all the Detroit dailies hoping to find at least a general mention of their endeavors to pay fitting tribute to the political genius of those who had founded our government. They were as usual doomed to disappointment. Only The Detroit News made a very brief mention of the Governor's visit. The other Detroit dailies entirely ignored that great event in the life of our city...

Let there be a divorce suit involving a Hamtramck public office holder— let there be a raid inspired by an outside politician seeking cheap publicity during the campaign for office—let there be a destruction of a campaign sign, and what happens? You read full columns adorned with suitable pictures of the "hoodlums and racketeers" of Hamtramck. In screaming headlines the world becomes "informed" by our exponents of "free speech and free press" about the social outcasts inferring by constant stress of such incidents that none but lawless people live in Hamtramck.

The *Detroit News* responded blandly, "The *News* regularly reports Hamtramck happenings which it considers of interest to its readers."

That provided little comfort to the aggrieved Hamtramckans. By then they should have been used to getting bad press. Through the years, Hamtramck was the subject of a host of local and even national stories that tended to paint the city as the most corrupt place this side of Al Capone's Chicago. Most of the bad stories were simply shrugged off. Yet occasionally, a nerve was struck.

In 1935, a consortium of nineteen organizations called the Inter-Organization Committee of Hamtramck launched an attack on the *Detroit Free Press* for a series of articles it ran on vice in Hamtramck.

In justice to our citizens, the articles should have pointed out that neither the Prosecuting Attorney nor the Sheriff of Wayne County has found any cause to complain about the conditions here, nor about the lack of cooperation. It should have been made clearer that the Prosecuting Attorney admits that all complaints forwarded by him to the Police Department were acted upon promptly.

In 1943, the common council threatened to sue *Time* magazine for an unfortunately accurate article on corruption in the school system. The council didn't challenge the facts of the story but was bitterly upset by the almost off-hand description by *Time* of Hamtramck as "a nest of factories, beer parlors and brothels entirely surrounded by Detroit." *Time* magazine attorney Richard I. Galland responded to the suit threat: "*Time* greatly regrets that the Council has misinterpreted the article to be derogatory toward the city and its population. Its purpose, rather, was to point up the indignation of the people of Hamtramck at the lowering of the standards of their school system which had once proved an example to other cities."

Time refused make a retraction.

Not all stories about Hamtramck were bad. In September 1948, the *Reader's Digest* carried the story, "Tennis Teacher Extraordinary," originally printed in *American Lawn Tennis* magazine. It told the tale of how legendary Hamtramck tennis coach Jean Hoxie trained champions. That same year, *Hit* magazine published a two-page spread about the prime acts performing at the Bowery night club, which was recognized as one of the finest—legitimate—night spots in the nation. And in August 1950, *Life* magazine ran an insightful photo essay on how a displaced Polish family found a new life, and home in Hamtramck. All those stories were positive representations about some aspect in Hamtramck. But you can bet they didn't sell as well as the stories on the latest beer bust or political Peyton Place saga.

Still, the press couldn't be blamed entirely for the bad publicity. After all, they didn't generate the scandals. But the fact that they relished such juicy morsels of sleaze angered many in the local population for its lack of balance.

In fact, Hamtramck from its earliest days had much to be proud of. The 1927 Public School Code—developed by Superintendent Maurice Keyworth along with Dr. Arthur B. Moehlman, professor of school administration and supervision of the University of Michigan's School of Education—is a prime example. It was a remarkably forward-thinking document. In essence, it outlined how to develop a successful school district, especially one with the unique challenges like Hamtramck, with its overwhelming immigrant population. The 260-page document details such wide-ranging topics as the organization of the school board and administration and how public relations can contribute to the success of the system. The school code was recognized as a landmark document and helped establish the Hamtramck Public School System as one of the finest in the nation. Districts across the country adopted portions of the school code. And Keyworth won so much respect for what he accomplished in Hamtramck that he was elected as state superintendent of public instruction in 1935. He likely would have rose to greater national prominence had he not been killed in an auto accident months after he left Hamtramck.

Emil Konopinski also had a positive association with Hamtramck Public Schools. The 1929 graduate of Hamtramck High was destined to a future

**In Memoriam
Dr. M. R. Keyworth**

Superintendent of Hamtramck Public Schools 1923 - 1935; State
Superintendent of Public Instruction, Elect 1935. Died June 22, 1935

Maurice Keyworth was Hamtramck schools superintendent from 1923 to 1935 and was responsible for creating the landmark Public School Code of 1927. It was a source of pride for the city.

on the assembly lines at Dodge Main to support his family when he was recognized by his teachers for his exceptional science and mathematical skills. Hamtramck High School principal E.M. Conklin went to the Hamtramck Rotary Club and arranged for Konopinski to receive a full scholarship to the University of Michigan, where he later distinguished himself as a physicist.

He soon rose to an elite circle of physicists and, ultimately, was part of the handful of them who were responsible for developing the atomic bomb in World War II. His job was to determine if detonating the bomb would set the atmosphere on fire.

John Hodiak was another memorable Hamtramck High School graduate. A member of the class of 1932, Hodiak went into acting and traveled to Chicago, New York and, eventually, Hollywood, where he became an A-list performer, starring in such films as Alfred Hitchcock's *Lifeboat*.

Also making a mark in Hollywood was Tom Tyler, a Dodge Main worker who got into body building, then acting and starred in a raft of "B" Westerns.

Tyler, born Vincent Markowski, was one of the top Western stars in the early 1940s. He also achieved great popularity as Captain Marvel, a hero of the serials. A favorite with the kids, Tyler routinely would come back to Hamtramck where he'd share cookies and milk with the local kids at the St. Anne's Community House. Forced into early retirement by illness, Tyler died in St. Francis Hospital on May 1, 1954, at age fifty.

Gail Kobe, another Hamtramck High School graduate, found great success as an actress, appearing in dozens of TV shows in the 1950s and 1960s. She achieved success behind the camera as well, producing such popular shows as *Peyton Place*.

In the world of athletics, Walter Roxey was an early wresting star, while Jean Hoxie took tennis champs Jane "Peaches" Bartkowicz and Fred Kovaleski to many national and international titles, including Wimbledon wins. Hamtramckans Tom Paciorek and Ike Blessitt played professional baseball, while Rudy Tomjanovich starred on the basketball court. In 1959, the Hamtramck Little League team won the world championship, and the Pony League team followed with a world title in 1961.

Whole books could be written about Hamtramck's association with the labor movement. The big Dodge Main strike of 1937 was instrumental in helping the United Auto Works win recognition as the voice of the auto workers. And regardless of Mary Zuk's affiliation with the Communist Party, she succeeded in carrying the message of anger and frustration of the people all the way to Washington—a powerful reach for a little woman from Hamtramck.

In 1936, Hamtramck completed one of it most important civic projects, the construction of the new football stadium that was almost immediately named Keyworth Stadium, in honor of Maurice Keyworth. Built as a Works Progress Administration project, its dedication was such a momentous event that President Franklin D. Roosevelt spoke at the ceremony.

A dozen years later, President Harry S. Truman made the first of a series of visits to Hamtramck. He marched down Jos. Campau to Veterans Park where he spoke to the enthusiastic crowds. Neither president was daunted by Hamtramck's wild reputation. In later years, Presidents John Kennedy,

Hamtramck's wild reputation didn't scare major politicians away. President Harry S. Truman visited the city in 1948. Looking away is Mayor Stephen Skrzycki. To the left is St. Florian's pastor, Father Peter P. Walkowizk. The other person isn't identified.

George H.W. Bush, Ronald Reagan and Bill Clinton would all pay visits to Hamtramck. And in perhaps the ultimate symbol of absolution, on September 19, 1987, Pope John Paul II came to Hamtramck.

All of these people played a positive role in Hamtramck's history. They stood in sharp counterpoint to the seamy side of life. Nor should it be thought that Hamtramck was corrupt from the foundation up. In fact, the vast majority of people in Hamtramck were no more than hardworking, honest, moral people. It was the poor Polish immigrants who sacrificed what little they had to build St. Florian Church, a magnificent English-Gothic structure that was so remarkable it won the American Architect Award in 1929. People who were paid extremely little gave what they had to support their church. That also was true with the African American community, which built a social structure supported by churches, strong family and ethnic ties. And they had to deal with the double disadvantage of being at the bottom of the social scale while coping with the racism that permeated America. In fact, most Hamtramckans were preoccupied with the day-to-day challenges of just surviving, not with breaking the law.

It's difficult to gauge how the average Hamtramck and Hamtramckan viewed all the shenanigans that were taking place around them. Some of it must have seemed rather amusing, such as the women who pushed baby buggies with false bottoms where the illegal hooch was stowed; some of it must have been exasperating, especially the endless parade of politicians who ran afoul of the law; some of it was deadly serious. None of it was a source of pride.

Signs that the general population was getting tired of the ongoing mess began to surface in the early 1940s. In the wake of the parking meter scandal and resignation of Mayor Kanar, the people were looking for political peace. They found it with candidates Raymond F. Matyniak and Dr. Stephen Skrzycki, who topped the city primary election in March 1942. The way was opened for both men when acting mayor Anthony Tenerowicz and director

God and government were always a part of the tapestry of Hamtramck. Here, veterans groups present flags and copies of the U.S. Constitution to students at St. Florian School.

of public safety Joseph Wisniewski, both veteran politicians, announced they would not run for office. Dr. Skrzycki was a medical doctor who practiced at St. Francis Hospital. He also had served on the school board in the 1930s, but he was never implicated in any questionable activity. Similarly, Matyniak had a clean record, having served as city controller.

Another break from past elections was a plea from the community that the political animosity be put aside.

"The need for a peaceful election campaign—devoid of mud-slinging, beer parties and the like—cannot be over emphasized," the *Citizen* newspaper wrote in a front-page editorial three weeks before the election. "Hamtramck has been the butt of outside criticism too long. That the city's two principal Mayoral candidates have openly announced their intentions to abide by ethical procedures is a most commendable undertaking."

And they did. The election of 1942 was one of the calmest in the city's history to that time—maybe even to this day.

"Election Seen In Many Years As Quietest" read the headline of the February 27, 1942 edition of the *Citizen*. "The two principal candidates— Raymond Matyniak and Dr. Stephen S. Skrzycki—have so far conducted clean campaigns in accordance with promises given when they announced their candidacies," the story related. Rather than attacking each other, Skrzycki focused his campaign on bringing clean government to Hamtramck. Matyniak ran on his record as city controller and promised to be a "full time mayor." This was a modest challenge to Skrzycki, who was an active physician. But the charge, such as it was, gave Skrzycki the opportunity to note how he could do more in a few hours than most people could do all day.

It worked. Skrzycki easily outdistanced Matyniak in the primary election by a margin of 5,335 to 3,203. The results told only part of the story. "Aside from the statistical facts concerning the election, by far the most outstanding feature was the serenity of the occasion," the *Citizen* wrote. "No campaign literature, no signs near booths, no political workers—nothing marred the day."

An accompanying front-page editorial called the election "a great day in Hamtramck's history." It went on: "It all happened because two candidates for the office of Mayor had decided, upon the urging of the people, to conduct a clean campaign. The candidates promised and came through with flying colors."

The results of the general election held a month later reflected the primary vote. Skrzycki won by a somewhat larger margin, 7,616 votes to Matyniak's 4,748. In addition, four new common council members and a new justice of the peace were elected. Another unusual aspect was that Skrzycki would take

Little Lessons in Courtesy

"You drink first, Virginia."

Published by Authority
BOARD OF EDUCATION
Hamtramck, Michigan

1929

Little Lessons in Courtesy was printed by the Hamtramck Public Schools in 1929 to help train the children to be responsible members of the community. The kids learned their lessons—often the adults did not.

office with a budget surplus. Not since 1923 had the city started a new fiscal year in the black. It was a promising beginning, and, indeed, it did reflect a genuine change in Hamtramck.

Skrzycki would win reelection to a then unprecedented five two-year terms. His administration was marked by a welcome blandness. In fact, he virtually campaigned on how scandal-free his years in office had been.

Skrzycki died in 1954, the first of Hamtramck's mayors to die. Thousands attended his funeral at St. Florian Church.

Corruption did not totally end with the arrival of Mayor Skrzycki, but illegal activity would never rise to the wild days of Hamtramck's early years as a city. Skrzycki in particular set a new tone for the city. From the point of his election, the headlines would be dominated with stories of the war effort, first focusing on bond sales, then gradually the rising report of casualties. After the war, Hamtramck underwent a major transformation, as the city's population began a serious decline. The men returning from the war had a very different view of what they wanted in life. They had a broader perspective, having seen the world under dreadful circumstances. The tight little surroundings of Hamtramck didn't offer enough room, so many began migrating to the suburbs, particularly Warren and beyond to Sterling Heights, Utica and Troy.

The ugly incidents that marred Hamtramck's political scene began to slip into history. There were flare-ups, of course. Blind pigs operated, some fairly openly, well into the 1960s. The Miller Restaurant, at 3038 Miller Street, was raided twice in seven months by police in 1965. And the little candy store on Lumpkin Street between Wyandotte and Geimer Streets—affectionately called Moldy Joe's by the neighborhood kids—was a known blind pig until it was demolished during the urban renewal programs of the 1960s.

And from time to time, various politicians would be linked to some questionable activity. But none rose to a level that would prompt a grand jury investigation or lead to any indictments. In fact, Hamtramck's political and social landscape for the most part became almost like any other city—not that any aspect of Hamtramck could really be characterized as routine.

What could be learned from all of this?

Not much, really. The wild days of Hamtramck were a reflection of a different time and different circumstances. People were drawn into corrupt activity by sex, money and the quest for power. That's hardly something that no longer occurs today at the highest levels of government.

It's the darker side of human nature. But it is all human.

Hamtramck weathered the wild times and came through as a stronger—if tamer—community. But it has lost none of its vibrancy—just its wicked ways.

Visit us at
www.historypress.net